BANNING WEAPONS OF MASS DESTRUCTION

BANNING WEAPONS OF MASS DESTRUCTION

FREDERICK N. MATTIS

PRAEGER SECURITY INTERNATIONAL
Westport, Connecticut • London

Library of Congress Cataloging-in-Publication Data
Mattis, Frederick N., 1951–
    Banning weapons of mass destruction / Frederick N. Mattis.
        p. cm.
    Includes bibliographical references and index.
    ISBN 978-0-313-36538-6 (alk. paper)
    1. Nuclear disarmament—International cooperation. 2. Nuclear arms
control—International cooperation. 3. Nuclear nonproliferation—International
cooperation. 4. Nuclear weapons—Government policy. 5. Weapons
of mass destruction—Government policy. I. Title.
JZ5675.M38   2009
327.1′745—dc22   2008047569

British Library Cataloguing in Publication Data is available.

Library of Congress Catalog Card Number: 2008047569
ISBN: 978-0-313-36538-6

First published in 2009

Praeger Security International, 88 Post Road West, Westport, CT 06881
An imprint of Greenwood Publishing Group, Inc.
www.praeger.com

Printed in the United States of America

The paper used in this book complies with the
Permanent Paper Standard issued by the National
Information Standards Organization (Z39.48–1984).

10 9 8 7 6 5 4 3 2 1

Contents

Acknowledgments   vii

Abbreviations   ix

Chapter 1. The Landscape of Nuclear Weapons   1

Chapter 2. Partial Measures—De-Alerting and No First Use   8

Chapter 3. Nuclear Ban Entry into Force   10

Chapter 4. Should Withdrawal Be Permitted?   17

Chapter 5. Verification, Disposition of HEU, and Reprocessing   22

Chapter 6. Problematic States   40

Chapter 7. Weapons Elimination   47

Chapter 8. Superseding Today's Non-Proliferation Treaty   52

Chapter 9. Prior Prohibition of Chemical and Biological Weapons   58

Chapter 10. Reservations   66

Chapter 11. Countering Near-Earth Objects   76

Chapter 12. Societal Verification   80

Chapter 13. Other Matters   84

Chapter 14. Summary   88

Appendix A: Analysis of the Model Nuclear Weapons Convention   93

Appendix B: 1968 Non-Proliferation Treaty   101

Appendix C: 1972 Biological Weapons Convention   107

Appendix D: 2005 Six-Party Joint Statement of Principles   112

Appendix E: Response to U.S. Rationale for Nuclear Weapons   114

Notes   117

Index   125

Acknowledgments

With respect to the writing of *Banning Weapons of Mass Destruction*, I offer my heartfelt thanks—

To my mother, Margaret, and my late father, Norman Mattis, for their example of striving for a better world;

To my wife, Nancy, for her cheerful and unflagging support over the years of this endeavor;

To my sister, Susan Mattis, for her valuable critical examination of the text, resulting in major and minor improvements;

To my brother-in-law, Joseph G. Shay, for his ready technical assistance in preparing the manuscript.

Abbreviations

BWC	Biological Weapons Convention
CANDU	Canadian deuterium-uranium
C.D.	Conference on Disarmament
CWC	Chemical Weapons Convention
CTBT	Comprehensive Test Ban Treaty
HEU	highly enriched uranium
IAEA	International Atomic Energy Agency
ICBM	intercontinental ballistic missile
LEU	low-enriched uranium
LTBT	Limited Test Ban Treaty
MNWC	Model Nuclear Weapons Convention
MOX	mixed-oxide plutonium-uranium fuel
NATO	North Atlantic Treaty Organization
NEAR	Near-Earth Asteroid Rendezvous
NEO	Near-Earth Object
NPT	Non-Proliferation Treaty
PNE	Peaceful Nuclear Explosion
SORT	Strategic Offensive Reductions Treaty (the Moscow Treaty)
SALT	Strategic Arms Limitation Talks
START	Strategic Arms Reduction Treaty
TNT	trinitrotoluene

The Landscape of Nuclear Weapons

Nuclear weapons are the supreme "weapons of mass destruction" although biological weapons are more often cited as being within terrorists' reach, based on relative ease of creation. Chemical weapons, which pose a lesser-scale danger to life and society than nuclear or even biological, round out the triumvirate of mass destruction weapons threatening humanity as instruments of war or terrorism.

Crude precursors of today's chemical and biological (chem-bio) weapons were used sporadically in premodern eras, whereas nuclear weapons only appeared with the first test explosion by the United States on July 16, 1945. The former Soviet Union initially tested nuclear weapons in 1949, Britain in 1952, France in 1960, and China in 1964. Since then, Israel (ca. 1967), India (1974), and Pakistan (ca. 1987) have attained nuclear weapons, and in 2006 the People's Democratic Republic of Korea (North Korea) conducted an underground test explosion.

Some countries signally chose an opposite course. After the 1991 collapse of the Soviet Union, former Soviet "republics" Ukraine, Kazakhstan, and Belarus renounced nuclear arms and by 1996 completed transfer of Soviet-era weapons to Russia for dismantling. South Africa in 1990–1991 dismantled its six surreptitiously created nuclear warheads, and in the 1970s and 1980s countries such as Taiwan (Republic of China), Algeria, Argentina, and Brazil turned away from their reputed aspirations for nuclear arsenals. More recently, Libya in December 2003 credibly renounced possession and pursuit of nuclear and chem-bio weapons.

Of the world's estimated 21,000 nuclear warheads, about 95 percent are possessed by the Russian Federation and the United States. The bilateral 2002 Strategic Offensive Reductions Treaty (SORT) or "Moscow Treaty" stipulates reduction of *deployed* strategic nuclear warheads to a maximum of 2,200 for each side at the end of 2012. The Moscow Treaty does not, however, require the dismantling of those U.S. and Russian warheads taken off deployment.

The treaty also permits either party to withdraw and prescribes no stages of reduction before the final result. Moreover, the deadline of December 31, 2012, for reduced deployments to be in effect is also the date of treaty expiration, so thereafter the United States or Russia could expand deployed forces once again (although this is most unlikely, as is pre-2012 withdrawal by either party).

The Moscow Treaty's extreme brevity, three pages, reflects the lack of verification provisions (although both sides later agreed to use established Strategic Arms Reduction Treaty or START procedures), as does the lack of required dismantling of newly nondeployed warheads and the lack of phased reduction in deployments before the mandated result at the end of 2012. The Moscow Treaty supplanted the START process; START I and II were negotiated, but only START I (signed 1991), which limited "accountable" deployed strategic warheads to 6,000 per side by December 5, 2001, came into effect.

Other than strategic nuclear weapons, the majority of U.S. and Russian (Soviet) nonstrategic or "tactical" weapons were retired from deployment in 1991 by the initiative of President G. H. W. Bush, with reciprocal actions by Soviet President Mikhail Gorbachev. The United States, for its part, eliminated 1,740 nuclear artillery shells and 1,250 short-range nuclear missiles and withdrew a combined 1,850 nuclear bombs and cruise missiles from land-based naval aircraft, naval surface ships, aircraft carriers, and attack submarines. The major draw-downs notwithstanding, the United States at present maintains (over the objections of Russia) an estimated total of 240 nuclear warheads at airbases in Belgium, Britain, Germany, Italy, the Netherlands, and Turkey.

Today's Russian and U.S. nuclear arsenals have their source in decades of mistrust and hostility. U.S. suspicions of Soviet geopolitical intentions had emerged by the end of World War II, spurring the United States to continue its postwar nuclear program before the Soviet Union became a nuclear power in 1949. The United States also first developed and tested (1952) the thermonuclear or "hydrogen" bomb (a 1 megaton such weapon would destroy or substantially damage by blast effects an area six to seven times that of the Hiroshima detonation). During the Cold War, the Soviets blamed the West for the arms race but tended to balk—especially earlier on—at serious consideration of arms control measures requiring inspection, ostensibly out of concern that inspection would mean spying on the Soviets and discovering weaknesses that the West could exploit in war. A Cold War vignette holds a mirror to the unease generated by massive nuclear arsenals in the hands of "geopolitical enemies": American public opinion in 1956 responded positively to presidential candidate Adlai Stevenson's support for a ban on atmospheric nuclear tests; but when the *Soviets* praised the proposal, it was (in *Newsweek's* words) a "political kiss of death" for Stevenson.[1]

Few if any Western observers today believe that Russia harbors deathly ambitions to conquer Western Europe or the United States. Certainly, those American military leaders who over the years have advocated nuclear weapons have not sought the destruction of Russia in war, as underscored by retired Air

Force General Lee Butler's remark that he finds he must "struggle constantly with the task of articulating my convictions [opposing nuclear weapons] without denigrating or diminishing the motives and sacrifice of countless colleagues."[2] General Butler was joined by 61 other retired generals and admirals worldwide in releasing a statement on December 5, 1996, which said in part:

> We, military professionals who have devoted our lives to the national security of our countries and our peoples, are convinced that the continuing existence of nuclear weapons in the hands of the nuclear powers, and the ever-present threat of the acquisition of these weapons by others, constitutes a peril to global peace and security and to the safety and survival of the people we are dedicated to protect.[3]

"Others" adverts to terrorists as well as states—and it is only by abolishing the nuclear arsenals of states that the avenue of potential terrorist warhead acquisition by theft or diversion will be eliminated.

Even after implementation of the 2002 Moscow Treaty, with its limit at the end of 2012 of 2,200 deployed strategic warheads per side, that number does not include nonstrategic nuclear weapons nor additional strategic warheads held "in reserve." Other states' arsenals are much smaller, with China estimated (with much uncertainty) to possess some 200 weapons (missile warheads plus freestanding or "gravity" bombs), France 300–350, Britain just under 200, Israel 75–300, India perhaps 40–50, Pakistan 25–50, and North Korea a likely 5–10. Fortunately, at least a few dozen additional states that are capable of producing nuclear weapons have refrained from stepping down that path.

Nuclear weapons, which are indeed the most widely, reliably, and variously destructive of any class of weapons, are fabricated based on either "gun-assembly" or "implosion." The latter technique is by far the more complex, utilizing conventional (chemical) high explosives precisely configured as lenses around a fissile material core of plutonium or highly enriched uranium (HEU). Detonation of the explosives squeezes the nuclear material, effecting supercriticality and, in conjunction with a neutron source engineered in the bomb, a "splitting the atom" chain reaction. Massive amounts of energy are released, as quantified in Einstein's famous equation. With the simpler "gun" design, a fission chain reaction results when masses of HEU are suddenly brought together, using chemical explosive as propellant, in an elongated container (only up to 2 percent of the HEU undergoes fission before a gun weapon explodes). Neutron emission from plutonium, which would preinitiate fission and cause the explosion to "fizzle," precludes the use of plutonium in gun weapons, whereas HEU is suitable for both types.

Although the engineering of an implosion weapon is quite difficult, the only major challenge for an HEU gun weapon is enrichment of uranium—which is widely regarded as beyond the capacity of terrorists. But if terrorists ever *acquired* 120 pounds of a state's uranium already enriched to 80 percent or greater uranium-235, then a gun-type bomb almost certainly could be built.

The terrorists easily could purchase needed equipment, including a precision lathe and vacuum furnace, and would need to employ the services of a rogue physicist, metallurgist, lathe operator, and electrical engineer. (A conclusion, detailed in chapter 5, is that elimination of HEU stocks is integral to a nuclear weapons ban.)

The heavy element uranium in nature is 99.3 percent isotope uranium-238 and only 0.7 percent weapons-usable, readily-fissionable isotope uranium-235.[4] To produce warhead material, the compound uranium hexafluoride in its gaseous state is laboriously "enriched," typically to 90 percent or greater uranium-235, by centrifuge, diffusion, or other technology. (Uranium enrichment—separation and concentration of isotope uranium-235—to 5 percent or less provides fuel for most of the world's nuclear power reactors and is not bomb material.[5]) The enriched uranium is then condensed to a solid and ultimately used as nuclear reactor fuel or, if high uranium-235 enrichments are produced, possibly as the explosive core of a nuclear weapon (see chapter 5 for discussion of two other current applications of HEU: fuel for some research reactors and a majority of naval propulsion reactors).

Uranium fission is the same phenomenon in nuclear warheads or reactors. Absorption of a striking neutron by a uranium-235 atom creates unstable uranium-236, which oscillates and instantly attenuates the binding, short-range "strong nuclear force." Electric force—repulsion between like-charge protons—thus is unimpeded and splits apart the nucleus, with a slight net loss of mass. Neutrons released during the fission may initiate a chain reaction of fissions either controlled (reactor) or explosively uncontrolled (warhead). Along with energy and neutron release, the reaction yields highly radioactive "fission products." (In nuclear power plant reactors, the energy of darting fission products in collision with other atoms provides heat that changes water to steam, which drives a turbine-generator system to produce electricity.)

Historically, plutonium rather than HEU has been used in the majority of warheads, because HEU is costlier to produce; also, the more efficient fissionability of plutonium allows warheads on missiles to be smaller and lighter. Plutonium's existence is contingent on bombardment by neutrons of the common uranium isotope (238), as in a nuclear reactor. Capture of a neutron by uranium-238 creates unstable uranium-239, which decays to neptunium-239 and then to plutonium-239, an exceedingly toxic substance with a half-life of 24,000 years.

Operation of a nuclear reactor creates various plutonium isotopes. For production of military or weapons-grade plutonium of nearly pure isotope plutonium-239, uranium fuel in a reactor is irradiated for a relatively short time before unloading. The irradiated fuel is then chemically dissolved in nitric acid, the plutonium is extracted, further processed, and converted to metallic form (the most suitable for weapons). Non-weapons-grade plutonium builds up during the normal course of reactor operations, as at nuclear power plants, and contains a greater concentration of isotopes, such as plutonium-240, that are prone to spontaneous fission. Non-weapons-grade plutonium, however, is usable for nuclear weapons despite greater difficulty and hazard in its handling and less certainty of full performance in a detonation. (States, as a rule, use safer and more-efficient weapons-grade plutonium of 94 percent or greater plutonium-239.)

In a "boosted" nuclear weapon, heat and pressure from a fission detonation triggers fusion of relatively small amounts of hydrogen isotopes deuterium and tritium, to provide more neutrons for fissioning the nuclei of more plutonium or HEU atoms. In a thermonuclear or "hydrogen" bomb, radiation pressure from a fission detonation triggers fusion of large amounts of hydrogen isotopes, with explosion of stupendous destructive force. Much of this energy release in many thermonuclear weapons results from fusion-released neutrons fissioning the atoms of the uranium-material bomb-fuel casing, so those weapons derive their awesome yield directly from fission as well as fusion—the latter of which also powers the sun, life's fundamental energy source.

Nuclear weapons produce an extraordinary blast wave and an inferno of fire and heat plus radiation, including concrete-penetrating gamma rays. Radiation exposure in humans gives rise to burns, hemorrhage, diseases, death, cancer, and mutations and illnesses in future generations. Radioactive particles, sucked up by the massive mushroom cloud, are deposited as high as the stratosphere and may settle onto Earth and work through the food chain months or even years later.

The following account, by Nagasaki Mayor Iccho Itoh at the International Court of Justice (the World Court) on November 7, 1996, is not intended here as a stark animadversion on the atomic bomb decision and detonations in August 1945, but rather to emphasize the imperative that humanity's future includes no use of nuclear weapons:

> The explosion of the Nagasaki atomic bomb generated an enormous fireball, 200 meters in radius. The next instant, a ferocious blast and wave of heat assailed the ground with a thunderous roar. The surface temperature of the fireball was about 7,000 degrees C, and the heat rays that reached the ground were over 3,000 degrees C. The explosion instantly killed or injured people within a two-kilometer radius of the hypocenter, leaving innumerable corpses charred like clumps of charcoal and scattered in the ruins. In some cases not even a trace of the person's remains could be found. A wind of over 300 miles per hour slapped down trees and demolished most buildings. Even iron-reinforced concrete structures were so badly damaged that they seemed to have been smashed by a giant hammer. The fierce flash of heat, meanwhile, melted glass and left metal objects contorted like strands of taffy, and the subsequent fire burned the ruins of the city to ashes. The city of Nagasaki became a city of death where not even the sounds of insects could be heard.
>
> After a while, countless men, women and children began to gather for a drink of water at the banks of the nearby river, their hair and clothing scorched and their burnt skin hanging off in sheets like rags. Begging for help, they died one after another in the water or in heaps on the banks. Then radiation began to take its toll, killing

people like a scourge of death expanding in concentric circles from the hypocenter. Four months after the atomic bombing, 74,000 people were dead and 75,000 had suffered injuries, that is, two-thirds of the city population had fallen victim to this calamity that came upon Nagasaki like a preview of Apocalypse.

The approximately 21-kiloton explosion over Nagasaki, equivalent to 21,000 metric tons of TNT (trinitrotoluene), was a plutonium implosion device (as was the initial U.S. test) that delivered 5 to 10 percent the yield of typical strategic warheads today.[6] The Hiroshima detonation, using HEU and the previously untested, simpler "gun" design, was an estimated 12–15 kilotons. A relatively small, 20-kiloton air-burst nuclear weapon causes general destruction from blast effects over an area of 4–5 square miles. ("General" destruction denotes blast overpressure of greater than 5 pounds per square inch, enough to collapse wooden buildings.) A 1-megaton warhead explosion is equivalent to 1 million metric tons of TNT, with general destruction over 30-plus square miles and the range of thermal and radiation effects even greater.

The main international barrier to the spread of nuclear weapons is the 1968 Treaty on the Non-Proliferation of Nuclear Weapons, or Non-Proliferation Treaty (NPT). This milestone treaty entered into force with 43 parties in 1970 and now counts as its members all of the world's states, except for nuclear powers Israel, India, Pakistan, and NPT dropout North Korea. Given the treaty's Cold War inception, it is unsurprising that the NPT does *not* prohibit nuclear weapons to the five most-longstanding nuclear weapon states, a geopolitical chasm established in Article IX(3): "For the purposes of this treaty, a nuclear weapon State is one which has manufactured and exploded a nuclear weapon or other nuclear explosive device prior to January 1, 1967." NPT signatory states, in return for pledging to not develop or possess nuclear weapons (unless the state is one of the five nuclear weapon parties), are entitled to "peaceful" nuclear assistance under NPT Article IV(2):

> All the Parties to the Treaty undertake to facilitate, and have the right to participate in, the fullest possible exchange of equipment, materials and scientific and technological information for the peaceful uses of nuclear energy. Parties to the Treaty in a position to do so shall also cooperate in contributing alone or together with other States or international organizations to the further development of the applications of nuclear energy for peaceful purposes, especially in the territories of non-nuclear weapon States Party to the Treaty, with due consideration for the needs of the developing areas of the world.

This NPT provision is particularly germane to the five most longstanding, pre-1967 nuclear powers (Britain, China, France, Russia, and the United States) because they possess highly developed nuclear facilities and expertise. The NPT in Article X permits withdrawal by its parties upon provision of three months' notice, and consequently an NPT state could legally withdraw and then use previously acquired nuclear material, enhanced expertise, and technology to facilitate production of warhead quantities of HEU, or plutonium separated from irradiated reactor fuel.

"Permitted withdrawal" is only one of several problems (see chapter 8) of today's NPT as a vehicle for a nuclear weapons–free world. Despite deficiencies of the 1968 NPT, indefinite retention of that treaty may be held as favorable—on the view that "keeping the peace" has depended on nuclear possession by the five NPT nuclear weapon states, or at least the three in the Western Hemisphere (Britain, France, and the United States). In response to this view: irrespective of nuclear weapons, post-1945 bulwarks against the outbreak of "major wars" include the (1) lessons of suffering of World War II, (2) victory of heroic Allied forces over Fascism, (3) existence of the United Nations and its Security Council, (4) internationalization of trade, (5) 1991 dissolution of the Soviet Union, and (6) worldwide increase of human-to-human contacts with transportation, communication, and cultural exchange developments. Also important in many eyes is the conventional, non-nuclear military strength of the United States and allied countries, which has rendered the rise of a widely aggressive superstate almost inconceivable.

Border or localized hostilities, however, do pose a genuine nuclear danger. If nuclear weapons proliferate, relatively minor clashes could escalate without mercy into the reality of nuclear war. Another grim scenario is an attempted "preemptive" attack on a state's nuclear arsenal or facilities proving less than successful, and provoking a brief but terrible nuclear counterattack.

The threat of nuclear attainment by terrorists is also a peril to our lives—and to our democratic freedoms. This risk will remain unacceptably high unless and until the world's nuclear powers eliminate their nuclear stockpiles, and all states in possession of HEU blend it down to low-enriched uranium (LEU). The mere existence of the weapons in states' arsenals and the material (HEU) to create a nuclear weapon with relative ease entails a danger of theft or other means of acquisition by malignant terrorists.

The putative value of nuclear arsenals pales before the benefits of a world devoid of these weapons: freedom from nuclear attack and nuclear war, freedom from "false-alarm" nuclear strike (see chapter 2), elimination of risk that terrorists could acquire a bomb from a state's arsenal, and elimination (or virtually so) of the risk of terrorist bomb creation (see discussion in chapter 5).

Although nuclear weapons are the most massively and reliably lethal of armaments, biological and chemical weapons also demand address. For prohibition of these latter instruments of inhumanity, two treaties or "conventions" in parlance already exist: the 1972 Biological Weapons Convention (BWC) and the 1993 Chemical Weapons Convention (CWC)—both of which the United States and most other countries have already joined. Extension of these important agreements so they are truly "worldwide" is explored in chapter 9, and the reader is asked to hold until then the question, "What about biological and chemical weapons?"

Partial Measures—De-Alerting and No First Use

The rationale for implementation of "de-alerting" is to reduce or even fore-close the possibility of an inadequately considered, unauthorized, or false-alarm missile launch.[1] It would be the ultimate tragic irony if nuclear conflagration engulfed the earth—caused by technological "glitch" or human error that resulted in an immediate counterlaunch to a perceived attack, and such a full-scale, immediate response is only possible because of the high-alert status of many U.S and Russian missiles. Certainly, safeguards against this calamity exist on both sides, but men and machines are not perfect, and the payloads of intercontinental ballistic missiles (ICBMs) travel at 4 miles per second, and their accuracy is 100–300 yards "circular area probable," or the distance from which (on average) half of the weapons will fall.

A modicum of de-alerting has already been accomplished. In 1991 the United States and the Soviet Union de-alerted several hundred of their ICBMs, and in January 1994 the two countries announced the minor but welcome step of target-ing strategic weapons at the open oceans (this is a minor achievement, however, because a change to preprogrammed wartime target coordinates takes only a few minutes or less, depending on missile type). Also, U.S. and Russian bombers no longer routinely carry nuclear weapons; but bombers are just one leg of the two countries' strategic triad, along with land- and submarine-based missiles.

Measures such as the placement in (retrievable) storage of bombers' nuclear payloads are founded on U.S.-Russian safety concerns over nuclear weapons. However, significant de-alerting of all or nearly all U.S.-Russian deployed stra-tegic weapons is not yet in view; and even if, with the passage of time, only a relatively small number of massively powerful missiles remain on high alert, their impetuous or a false-alarm launch would wreak incalculable destruction.

De-alerting proponents point out that a nuclear response would have the same devastating effect on an attacker whether the response was delivered im-mediately by weapons on high alert, or hours or perhaps a day later, after acti-vation of de-alerted weapons. Notably, a single U.S. Trident II submarine is an invulnerable entity when submerged at sea and carries about 200 thermonuclear warheads, more than enough to cause hellish destruction and loss across any country.

Even assuming that "global" de-alerting of nuclear weapons is achieved, it will be no panacea because it will not eliminate nuclear warheads nor prohibit their possession worldwide, which is the key to liberation from the dangers posed by nuclear weapons. De-alerting of extant arsenals also does not solve the problem of nuclear proliferation to other states, nor does it eliminate today's pall of risk that terrorists could acquire a warhead from a state by theft or other means.

Any future U.S.-Russian de-alerting measures will likely be distinctly incremental, whereas the pledge of No First Use could be fully realized at any time. Only China of the five most-longstanding nuclear weapon states has a declared No First Use policy, dating to 1964. In 1982 the former Soviet Union also proclaimed No First Use, but in 1993 Russia rescinded this stance. Russia's backsliding on No First Use was presumably linked to its then-deterioration of Russian non-nuclear forces, Russian misgivings about the expansion of the North Atlantic Treaty Organization (NATO), and the years-long failure of the three Western nuclear powers to proclaim No First Use.

Will the United States and the other nuclear powers eschew the option of First Use of nuclear weapons in the near future? Historically, First Use in the United States has been envisioned primarily as a needed response to an "overwhelming conventional Soviet attack" on Western Europe; but today the Soviet Union has dissolved, and no assemblage of Warsaw Pact countries is confronting NATO, and the Russian military is not poised or prepared to attempt to overrun Western Europe. (Reference here to a feared "Soviet attack" is not to imply that the Soviets regarded with equanimity the prospect of starting World War III by an invasion of NATO countries, or that the Soviets would have invaded if nuclear weapons had not been invented.)

If, though, nuclear weapons are to possess the alleged utility of deterring some future aggression, then manifestly the possibility, or a perceived possibility, must exist that the weapons *may be used*. On this ground, the United States adheres to the thread of belief or conception that the ongoing U.S. option of possible First Use will prevent aggression or war from breaking out. Yet, consider the following instances: invading, culpable North Korea maintained its fight against forces from nuclear-armed countries in the Korean War; U.S., British, and French nuclear possession did not deter Saddam Hussein from temporarily seizing Kuwait in the 1991 Gulf War; an Argentine regime attempted to seize the Falklands (the *Malvinas*) in 1982 from nuclear power Britain; and the United States did not use its nuclear weapons in Vietnam.

The prospect of *any* use of nuclear weapons will become moot if they are eliminated by the vehicle of an international treaty that replaces today's inadequate (1968) NPT—with its provisions such as designation of pre-1967 nuclear powers as NPT nuclear weapon states. Chapter 3 focuses on the foundational question of "entry into force" of a new treaty.

Nuclear Ban Entry into Force

The criterion for entry into force of a viable nuclear weapons ban treaty can be determined by extrapolation from the world effort to prohibit nuclear test explosions. In 1963, with the Cuban Missile Crisis fresh in memory, a breakthrough occurred upon introduction of the Treaty Banning Nuclear Weapons Tests in the Atmosphere, in Outer Space and Under Water, or the Limited Test Ban Treaty (LTBT). The Preamble to the LTBT notes that its drafting parties (Britain, Soviet Union, and the United States) in formulating the Limited Test Ban were taking a step toward achieving "the discontinuance of all test explosions of nuclear weapons for all time, determined to continue negotiations toward this end, and desiring to put an end to the contamination of man's environment by radioactive substances." The 1963 treaty was "limited" because it did not prohibit underground tests. (In 1974 the United States and the Soviet Union signed the Threshold Test Ban Treaty, limiting their future underground tests to 150 kilotons; many of today's strategic warheads are 300- to 750-kiloton yield.)

Communist China initially denounced the 1963 LTBT as a ploy by the United States and the Soviet Union to impose pressure on countries such as China not to develop the bomb, so China would remain indefinitely in a subservient position to the ambitions of imperialism and errancies of Soviet communism. China, though, did pledge No First Use (upon 1964 attainment of nuclear weapons), and in 1996 China proclaimed, "We always stand for the complete prohibition and thorough destruction of nuclear weapons."[1]

China continued atmospheric test explosions until 1980 and France until 1974, whereas Britain, the United States, and the Soviet Union renounced such highly contaminative testing with the 1963 LTBT. In 1996, 33 years after the LTBT's introduction, the laboriously wrought Comprehensive Test Ban Treaty (CTBT) was opened for signature by states. The CTBT bars its parties from conducting underground as well as nonunderground test explosions and establishes an international network of seismic and other monitoring technologies.

The entry-into-force provision of the CTBT requires accession to the treaty by 44 specified countries with nuclear reactors. Neighboring India and Pakistan, having spurned the CTBT when it was opened for signature in 1996, subsequent to their May 1998 nuclear tests said they would *consider* signing. (As of mid-2008 the two countries have not signed and have given no fresh indication of intentions to do so.)

The United States to date has only signed (1996) and not yet ratified the CTBT, but the United States, interestingly and to its credit, is continuing its financial support for the treaty-monitoring regime. Whatever the eventual fate of official entry into force of the treaty, the current moratorium on test detonations may well endure due to the normative force of the CTBT, even without its official entry into force. However, a state of mid-level industrial attainment could successfully create nuclear weapons of the HEU gun type without conducting an explosive test. As already noted, the only major technological challenge to manufacture a gun weapon is enrichment of uranium in isotope-235. (In early 2004, Pakistani nuclear avatar A. Q. Khan scandalously admitted his leading role in a network of suppliers and contacts that provided uranium-enrichment technology and nuclear secrets to the Islamic Republic of Iran, Libya, and North Korea.)

In October 1999, a CTBT-authorized international conference was held in an attempt to hasten, without violating principles of international law, entry into force of the CTBT. But the test ban treaty's entry-into-force requirement is clearly stated, so the conference could only hold discussions and adopt a 10-point document urging states to join. If and when accession to the treaty by all 44 treaty-named countries is achieved, then the CTBT officially will come into effect for its parties, that is, the 44 plus others that have joined. Because India and Pakistan share a history of tension and have not signed the CTBT, the two countries nuclear postures merit discussion.

When international outcry greeted the nuclear tests by India and Pakistan in May 1998, India followed its pattern of expressing umbrage that states with nuclear arsenals are prone to criticize development of such by other states. If criticized by nuclear powers for proliferation, India can retort, "Why should you have a monopoly? We're a sovereign country too." Another riposte could spotlight the disparity between the 11 combined Indo-Pakistani underground detonations in 1998 and the 2,046 collective test explosions by today's five NPT nuclear weapon states from 1945 to 1996, an average of one every nine days. (None of those five states has tested post-1996, and only France and China did so after 1992.)

In May 1998, India's Prime Minister A. Vajpayee declared, "We live in a world where India is surrounded by nuclear weaponry [of China and Pakistan]. The world community should appreciate the fact that India, the second-most populous country on Earth, waited for five decades [after independence] before taking this step."[2] (Left unsaid is that India tested, and labeled as a "peaceful" explosion, a nuclear device in 1974.[3]) Seismic monitoring indicated that the largest 1998 India test blast was approximately of Hiroshima size, whereas India claimed a top test yield of about triple that—43 kilotons.

The rationale that one's country is "surrounded by" or otherwise subject to a nuclear threat could not be used under a worldwide elimination of nuclear weapons. The U.S. Department of Defense has observed, "The consequences of nuclear war between India and Pakistan would be catastrophic, both in terms of loss of life and in lowering the threshold for nuclear war in other parts of the world, particularly the adjacent Middle East/North Africa region."[4]

India's principal secretary to the prime minister in 1998 responded to criticism of India as follows:

India has taken many initiatives in the past for the elimination of all nuclear weapons. It is our regret that these proposals did not receive a positive response from the other nuclear weapon states. Had their response been positive, India need not have gone for the [May 1998] tests. This is where our approach to nuclear weapons is different from others. This difference is the cornerstone of our nuclear doctrine. It is marked by restraint and striving for the total elimination of all weapons of mass destruction. We have been and we will continue to be in the forefront of the calls for opening negotiations for a Nuclear Weapons Convention [treaty], so that this challenge can be dealt with in the same manner that we have dealt with the scourge of two other weapons of mass destruction, through comprehensive, universal and non-discriminatory treaties.[5]

The "two other weapons of mass destruction" have indeed been formally renounced by India and many other states, but not all states are likewise parties to the extant chemical and biological bans (see chapter 9 for nuclear ban treaty provision requiring accession by states to the chem-bio bans before signing the proposed nuclear ban treaty).

Pakistan for years has pursued nuclear weapons and advanced missile technology, while accusing much-larger India of hegemonic ambitions and falsely portraying China as a threat to India. Pakistan avers, and understandably so, that it cannot renounce nuclear weapons unless India does, but India quite likely will maintain its arsenal until nuclear weapons are eliminated worldwide (especially with respect to China; India's aforementioned, so-called peaceful nuclear explosion in 1974 was most probably in response to neighboring China's possession since 1964). India's nuclear possession may be bolstered by the concept that membership in the "nuclear club" brings stature to a state; but such thinking would lose its influence and even its meaning in a world without the weapons.

Similarly lost and departed would be the logic and basis asserted by a Pakistani spokesperson in defense of his country's nuclear weapons program: "India's nuclear capability continues to pose a serious threat to its neighbors, particularly Pakistan. It therefore became imperative for Pakistan to develop a minimal deterrent capability."[6] Although the underground nuclear test blasts by India and Pakistan in May 1998 were apparently significantly "successful," neither country has moved to sign the CTBT.

The CTBT's entry-into-force requirement of accession by 44 treaty-designated states with nuclear reactors gives legal stamp to the view that states indigenously capable of amassing plutonium should and must join the CTBT before its entry into force. Such states could with reason also seek to attain uranium-enrichment facilities, to produce LEU for reactor fuel—or HEU, readily usable in a "simple" gun-type or an implosion nuclear weapon (see chapter 5 for question of HEU disposition under worldwide prohibition of nuclear weapons).

As a main condition for eliminating nuclear weapons, the United States and other nuclear powers inevitably will insist that a nuclear ban treaty go a step further than the CTBT and *only enter into force after all states have joined.* Prohibition of test explosions under the CTBT is less portentous than elimination of nuclear weapons under a new treaty, and the latter will require agreement by all states. If to the contrary unanimity was not required for treaty entry into force, then a nonsignatory state might undertake development of nuclear weapons and could do so with a façade of guilelessness (because the state had not renounced the weapons by joining the treaty).

Unanimity before entry into force of the nuclear ban treaty must be true unanimity. For example, both Koreas would have to join, as would China and Taiwan (see chapter 6 for discussion of problematic states, such as North Korea).

With unanimous accession by states required before entry into force, how does the treaty account for an area that is attempting to secede or a chaotic area with no real, established state in governance? How is "unanimous accession to the treaty" to be determined, particularly when some areas may be in flux? "All states" cannot simply be listed in the treaty text as necessary parties for entry into force, because a bona fide state or states might emerge in the duration between opening for signature of the treaty and its entry into force (after unanimous accession is achieved).

The solution proposed here centers on a treaty provision whereby signatories convey their request that the U.N. Secretary-General announce when, in his or her judgment, "all states" have acceded to the treaty. By treaty terms, the date of this announcement marks the onset of a 180-day interval, the first 60 days of which are available for any state to publicly object to treaty entry into force and thereby *automatically delay it.* For example, an objection might be raised that "Area X is functioning independently of any real state's control and is, we believe, ambitious to develop nuclear weapons. Therefore, the nuclear ban treaty should not enter into force at this time" (in effect, until circumstances or perceptions change to an extent that the objecting state withdraws its call for delay). Or, an objection may be lodged along this line: "Area Y is, we believe, manifestly a state, but it has not joined the treaty." The U.N. Secretary-General's role is not to declare the nuclear treaty's actual entry into force but rather, by announcement of unanimous accession, to set in progress the 180-day interval leading to entry into force—unless rescinded by a state's objection within the first 60 days. The provision for rescission is without precedent, although an analogous interval is found in other treaties and allows signatories time for final preparations for compliance.

There may be concern that the U.N. Secretary-General's announcement that "all states" have joined could lend status to one or more governing regimes that are widely regarded as illegitimate. However, the Secretary-General's announcement need not make reference to which individual states have joined, but simply proclaim that all have done so. The announcement therefore would not authenticate any state's particular governing regime; however, if all states in the world's eyes had not joined, then it is foreseeable that a state or states would object to the treaty's entry into force (until circumstances or perceptions thereof satisfactorily have changed).

Positing an occurrence of objection to entry into force, let it be further posited that in three months' time the situation of concern was resolved and the state withdrew its objection. At that juncture, a 180-day interval toward official entry into force would begin again, raising the question of whether states would be able to object within the first 60 days of such a new interval and thereby rescind it. The answer must be affirmative, because it is possible that a nonsignatory "new state," or a serious geographical ambiguity, may appear during the three months of the posited first objection. *Another* state, not the first objector, might object with respect to circumstances that have arisen during the three months, and the right to do so should not be denied.

Although objection and consequent delay of treaty entry into force is possible, its likelihood is low for several reasons. First, the treaty would have been joined unanimously, as declared by the U.N. Secretary-General and thereby indicating the desire of the world to rid itself of threatening nuclear weapons. Second, the Secretary-General in all probability would refrain from declaring that "all states" had joined if any relevant and significant geopolitical ambiguity existed that could provide a basis for a state's objection. Third, a state's delay of entry into force without defensible cause would subject that state to intense international criticism; and a defensible cause is improbable, with any new or emergent state almost certainly being eager to demonstrate or solidify internationally its "state" status by avoiding suspicious nuclear activity and promptly acceding to the treaty joined by all other states. Fourth, in general, the world's tragically chaotic or largely "ungoverned" areas do not have the resources to realistically aspire to production of plutonium (using a nuclear reactor) or HEU for warheads. Given that fact, however, today's potential "loose nukes" avenue of warhead acquisition will not be closed off until all states eliminate their arsenals.

Inclusion in the proposed nuclear ban treaty of a state's prerogative to delay, without limitation of time, entry into force is insufficient to gain accession by all states. Another beckoning provision stipulates that once unanimity and official entry into force is attained, the treaty's prohibition of nuclear weapons *applies everywhere*. This would prevent any nascent, "breakaway," or future state from proclaiming, "We didn't sign it, so we're not bound by it," without confronting worldwide condemnation and other forms of opposition. The prohibition of nuclear weapons to future states is necessary to gain accession by all current states, and it is justified by the unanimity achieved before entry into force. As with many extant treaties, the proposed nuclear ban treaty is of unlimited duration, which combined with the prohibition of nuclear weapons everywhere forbids nascent or future states from undertaking treaty-barred activities (see also chapter 4, on "nonwithdrawal").

The process whereby a state becomes party to a treaty may extend to months or even years. In the United States, a satisfactorily negotiated treaty is signed by the executive branch and then debated in Congress. A vote on ratification is eventually taken in the Senate, requiring two-thirds majority of senators present and voting for treaty approval; if attained, a document of formal U.S. accession to the treaty is transmitted to the treaty depositary (which acts as safekeeper and distributor of membership documents). To ban nuclear weapons, when would an individual country be bound by treaty terms? The evident alternatives are as follows: upon signing, ratifying, formally acceding, or when official entry into force occurs (six months after all states have joined, in the absence of objection by a state and consequent delay).

The guiding document for operation of treaties is the Vienna Convention on the Law of Treaties. Article 18 of the Convention reads in part:

> A State or an international organization is obliged to refrain from acts which would defeat the object and purpose of a treaty when (a) that State ... has signed the treaty or has exchanged instruments constituting the treaty subject to ratification ... until that State shall have made its intention clear not to become a party to the treaty; or (b) that State ... has expressed its consent to be bound by the treaty, pending the entry into force of the treaty and provided that such entry into force is not unduly delayed.

Section (b) is not problematic for banning nuclear weapons, because any state could of its own volition undertake to "consent to be bound" by the basic "object and purpose" of the prospective nuclear ban when the state signs or ratifies but before unanimous accession and entry into force. Section (a) *is* problematic, however, because its clear import is that when the United States, for example, signs a nuclear ban treaty, the United States must not flout the treaty's object and purpose from then on (unless the United States takes the drastic step of overtly renouncing intention to become a party). It is unrealistic, though, to think that the United States will abjure readiness and even possible use of nuclear weapons before all states doing so, and therefore the proposed treaty stipulates: "Notwithstanding Article 18(a) of the Vienna Convention on the Law of Treaties, signatories of this nuclear ban treaty have no express, implied, or tangential obligations under this treaty until it achieves unanimous accession and officially enters into force."

A nuclear weapon state certainly might, on its own initiative, accelerate or commence reduction of warheads after signing the treaty but before it enters into force. And today's NPT, already joined by about 95 percent of states as non-nuclear weapon parties (but with right of withdrawal), would remain in effect during the accumulation of all states as nuclear ban parties.

The abovementioned Law of Treaties' obligation of signatories to a treaty not to flout its "object and purpose" presupposes the beneficial intent of treaties. International law does not countenance disregard of a treaty's basic object and purpose by a state after it has become a treaty signatory but before enough states have joined for entry into force. This, though, needs to be excluded from applicability to the proposed worldwide nuclear ban, because the current nuclear powers will not obligate themselves to renounce their "option" to use nuclear weapons even one day before all states also renounce. A likely three or four years or so will be accorded to eliminate the weapons (see chapter 7), but prohibition of their use or threat of use applies from the date of treaty entry into force, which occurs (unless delayed because formal objection is lodged) 180 days after "all states" have joined, as announced by the U.N. Secretary-General.

Next is the critical question of withdrawal.

4

Should Withdrawal Be Permitted?

If withdrawal by parties from the enacted nuclear ban *is* permitted, then the current nuclear powers probably will not sign, in conformance with this logic:

> Suppose we join this treaty and proceed to eliminate our nuclear weapons, but Country X in the future exercises its right to legally withdraw from the treaty. Although we would probably also withdraw and redevelop some nuclear weapons, that would destroy the ban and destroy the security benefits of a world free of nuclear weapons. If states are permitted to withdraw, we won't sign, because nuclear weapons could with legal cover reemerge and proliferate at any time. Also, a state could use a mere threat of treaty-permitted withdrawal to create fear or instability.

Treaties, as a rule, do permit states to drop out, as in Article X(1) of today's NPT:

> Each party shall in exercising its national sovereignty have the right to withdraw from the Treaty if it decides that extraordinary events, related to the subject-matter of this Treaty, have jeopardized the supreme interests of its country. It shall give notice of such withdrawal to all other parties to the Treaty and to the United Nations Security Council three months in advance. Such notice shall include a statement of the extraordinary events it regards as having jeopardized its supreme interest.

States' capability to legally drop out of the NPT is a singular flaw if the goal is a world permanently free of nuclear weapons. But on the premise that *all states* join a new treaty banning nuclear weapons worldwide, it is inadvisable for "withdrawal" to be permitted, because withdrawal by a state would induce the same action by at least a few other states. (Notably, though, even in the venerable NPT the right of withdrawal is not "absolute" but qualified by the three months' notice requirement; so "nonwithdrawal" in a worldwide nuclear ban treaty is less a leap than it may initially appear.)

The 1968 NPT required only 43 parties for its entry into force (1970), and the treaty is still not joined by India, Pakistan, or Israel—and North Korea dropped out in January 2003. The NPT, lacking the equalizing stratum of unanimity, understandably permits withdrawal, insofar as a non-NPT state might at some time instigate a nuclear peril so threatening to an NPT non-nuclear weapon state that the latter would feel compelled to withdraw and develop its own nuclear arsenal.

Besides nonunanimity, a pillar of the ineluctability of a withdrawal provision in today's NPT is its Article IX(3) inclusion and warrant of NPT nuclear weapon states, or those five that exploded a nuclear weapon or device before 1967. With a new, worldwide nuclear ban treaty having no provision for nuclear weapon states, the treaty's equal treatment of its parties militates against the traditional perceived necessity of legally permitted withdrawal. The non-withdrawal provision may not be, in itself, an *absolute* guarantee against break-out, but the legal force of the provision adds to the assuredness of fealty to the treaty (along with the unprecedented unanimity of accession by states before treaty entry into force).

State sovereignty and the supreme interests of a state are the traditional reasons, as in the NPT, for permitting withdrawal from treaties. Yet just as sovereignty allows a state to decline to join a treaty with a nonwithdrawal provision, so sovereignty inherently allows a state to join such a treaty. Regarding supreme interests, one such interest of the world's states and people—elimination of nuclear weapons and their attendant threat—can in all likelihood be achieved only through a nuclear ban treaty with a nonwithdrawal provision, or else there would be too much psychological instability associated with the prospective ban. The weight of legal prohibition of withdrawal is needed and would powerfully complement the geopolitical weight of unanimity of accession by states and the treaty-adherent influence of the nuclear ban's benefits to all people and states.

A state might counter, "We do need the right to lawfully withdraw from a nuclear weapons ban, in case another state flouts the treaty by barring inspectors or developing nuclear weapons." How realistic, though, is fear of treaty noncompliance with respect to a treaty joined by all states before its entry into force or imposition of any obligations? The consequences of cheating on a unanimous treaty being uncovered by nuclear ban inspection (see chapter 5) or by citizen reporting (see chapter 12) would be immense. Similarly, if a state openly barred inspectors or announced, "We'll no longer abide by the treaty," the state would plunge itself into a maelstrom of worldwide excoriation, opposition, and economic boycott. The U.N. Security Council would meet and deliberate under its U.N. Charter Article 39 authority to "determine the existence of any threat to the peace, breach of the peace, or act of aggression and … make recommendations, or decide what measures shall be taken in accordance with Articles 41 and 42, to maintain or restore international peace and security." Article 41 empowers the Security Council

> to decide what measures not involving the use of armed force are to be employed to give effect to its decisions, and it may call upon the Members of the United Nations

to apply such measures. These may include complete or partial interruption of economic relations and of rail, sea, air, postal, telegraphic, radio, or other means of communication, and severance of diplomatic relations.

Article 42 of the Charter, which was the legal basis for U.N. authorization of military action in the Korean War and the 1991 Gulf War, states:

> Should the Security Council consider that measures provided for in Article 41 would be inadequate or have proved to be inadequate, it may take such action by air, sea or land forces as may be necessary to maintain or restore international peace and security. Such action may include demonstrations, blockade, and other operations by air, sea or land forces of Members of the United Nations.

It can be said to be difficult to imagine a greater motivation for warnings and action by the Security Council than a state barring inspectors or through other flagitious act breaking out of a nuclear weapons ban joined by all states. (If the Council was ineffectual or indecisive, action could be undertaken by NATO or a lone country such as the United States.)

The caveat may be raised that if a large nation broke out of the treaty, the U.N. Security Council might not take real action because of the offender's size or because prospective action could be vetoed by a permanent Security Council member that had broken out. Granted that may be true, but even a large state would face extreme criticism and related consequences from abroad, plus probable strong domestic opposition—the latter primarily because the treaty applies equally to all states. And on the positive side, states would have ample reason to comply with the treaty, for all people would share in the benefits of a nuclear weapons–free world.

The treaty's nonwithdrawal provision does not mean that if a state ever *did* breach the nuclear ban, other states would have no recourse for responding with the *temporary* development of nuclear weapons. The Vienna Convention on the Law of Treaties in Article 60(2) provides as follows:

> A material breach of a multilateral treaty by one of the parties entitles … : (a) a party specifically affected by the breach to invoke it as a ground for suspending the operation of the treaty in whole or in part in the relation between itself and the defaulting State … ; (b) any party other than the defaulting State … to invoke the breach as a ground for suspending the operation of the treaty in whole or in part with respect to itself if the treaty is of such a character that a material breach of its provisions by one party radically changes the position of every party with respect to the further performance of its obligations under the treaty.

With unanimous accession by states constituting the foundation and precondition ("character" above) of the nuclear ban treaty, Section (b) would apply, as well as Section (a). Therefore, if a state materially breached the treaty, the United States or other nations would have credible grounds to ignore the ban, but only temporarily because the treaty *does not permit withdrawal*. Once the material breach by the defaulting state has been fully rectified, another party's "suspension" of its treaty participation must end. This would occur unless a state decided, in effect if not by declaration, to disregard the treaty's nonwithdrawal provision. (Any such disregard would be met by worldwide condemnation, the prospect of which would be a deterrent to any unconscionable delay in return to full treaty participation.) The enacted nuclear ban treaty is always in force and could be legally disregarded, under color of Law of Treaties Article 60(2), by a party only if and while there is a prior, initial material breach of the treaty by another party.

Most states have a perennial aversion to nuclear weapons, so it is likely that only a handful of states would react to a material breach with their own nuclear developments. Furthermore, if it was a smaller state that flouted the treaty, the U.N. Security Council—backed by all states in opposition to the lone treaty violator—would be in a strong position to dispose of a genuine, developing threat without any states resorting to the re-creation of nuclear arsenals. This might involve the extremity of a non-nuclear "preemptive attack," but one of justification, given the import of nuclear weapons and the unanimity of states' accession to the nuclear ban treaty before its entry into force.

In the contingency of a state ever responding with nuclear development to an initial material breach by another state, the proposed nuclear ban treaty decrees that the former state must name the state that is in breach, and must do so *before undertaking an otherwise treaty-prohibited activity*. The world would thereby be put on notice that the "responding" state might develop nuclear weapons (provoked by another, specified state's initial material breach of the worldwide nuclear weapons ban). The treaty also requires any such responding state to publicly declare when it considers the initially defaulting state to no longer be in material breach, after which time the responding state again must comply with the ban, in accordance with its unlimited duration and nonwithdrawal provision.

The prerogative of individual states to determine on a state's own account the "existence" of another state's material breach cannot be gainsaid if the treaty is to achieve unanimous accession and enter into force. For banning nuclear weapons, countries such as the United States simply will not relinquish the ultimate determination of material breach to an outside, collective entity.

Conceivably, the in-force nuclear ban treaty could be maliciously undermined by a state declaring without basis another state to be in material breach. This would be most unlikely under a unanimous ban, because a state arraigning another of material breach without significant reason, and to appearances as a pretext for nuclear weapons development, *foreseeably* would face a similar level of opposition and outrage as a state that would venture to unilaterally flout the worldwide treaty.

Finally, what if a state made a "declaration" to its citizens to this effect?

There are possible future circumstances, *different from* treaty material breach by another state and that, although extremely unlikely to occur, might impel our nation to give notice to the world and then temporarily ignore the nuclear ban treaty until the situation is rectified or ameliorated.

Could a state actually say this and then proceed to join the treaty banning nuclear weapons? The answer is yes, because the statement would not be part of the state's official accession (see related discussion in chapter 10). Such a pronouncement essentially would be moot, because with *or without* such a statement a state *could* abjure the treaty—although militating against that course would be the profound inducement to treaty compliance of the legal force of the nonwithdrawal provision, the geopolitical force of accession by all states, and the psychological and moral force of the treaty's elimination of the nuclear threat to all states and people. But, what if a state made such a pronouncement (as above) *after* entry into force of the treaty? Doing so would draw criticism, but in essence it would be just an adumbration of a most unlikely, hypothetical future action, and therefore it would not signify that the state was in material breach of the treaty (which, if so, would provide justification for other states to ignore the treaty until rectification of the breach).

To summarize provisions discussed so far, the proposed treaty banning nuclear weapons is of unlimited duration and (1) requires unanimous signature, ratification, and formal accession by states before entry into force; (2) stipulates that entry into force will be delayed if a state objects within 60 days after the U.N. Secretary-General announces that "all states" have joined; (3) absolves signatories of any and all treaty-related obligations before official entry into force (but meanwhile today's NPT remains in effect); (4) proclaims that, once in force, the prohibition of nuclear weapons applies everywhere; and (5) does not permit withdrawal. Regarding nonwithdrawal, international treaty law would not proscribe a state from *temporarily* ignoring the worldwide ban on nuclear weapons if another state was guilty of a material breach. Under the terms of the nuclear ban, however, a state cannot pursue an otherwise treaty-prohibited activity before naming the treaty-violating state (and to avoid world castigation would need to present sufficient evidence to credit the charge).

Chapter 5 outlines current nuclear verification (inspection), as mandated by the NPT for its non-nuclear weapon states, and recommends additional elements for the proposed worldwide nuclear ban treaty. To succeed, nuclear ban verification must be rigorous but not so extreme as to be rejected by some states. Also discussed in chapter 5 are the matters, consequential to a verification regime, of disposition of HEU and "reprocessing" of spent nuclear fuel.[1]

It is crucial that all states would be equally subject to a genuine nuclear ban treaty. Therefore, no state could resist the implementation of treaty-specified inspection measures on the basis of "discriminatory" treaty terms, a charge often leveled at today's NPT—with its designation of pre-1967 nuclear powers as NPT nuclear weapon states (and those five states being exempt from NPT-required international safeguards on plutonium and enriched uranium).

Verification, Disposition of HEU, and Reprocessing

A sphere of plutonium the size of an orange, or HEU the size of a soccer ball, is sufficient quantity of nuclear material for a nuclear weapon, and today's worldwide stocks (mostly U.S. and Russian) of military plutonium and HEU in weapons and from dismantled weapons amounts to perhaps 1,400 tons. The current NPT does not require international material accountancy and surveillance or "safeguards" for the five NPT "nuclear weapon states"—nor of course for the non-NPT states, which are Israel, India, Pakistan, and since 2003 treaty dropout North Korea. (Some fissionable material of NPT nuclear weapon states has been "voluntarily offered" for placement under International Atomic Energy Agency [IAEA] safeguards, but this does not apply to military-sector material except for amounts declared "excess.")

The 95 percent of states that are NPT non-nuclear weapon parties are mandated by Article II of the NPT (see appendix B) to accept safeguards on any fissionable material they possess for peaceful use, as enunciated by the Vienna-based IAEA in its 1972 INFCIRC/153, "The Structure and Content of Agreements Between the International Atomic Energy Agency and States Required in Connection with the Treaty on the Non-Proliferation of Nuclear Weapons":

> 1. The Agreement [nuclear material safeguards agreement between a state party and the IAEA] should contain, in accordance with Article III(1) of the Treaty on the Non-Proliferation of Nuclear Weapons [Non-Proliferation Treaty—NPT], an undertaking by the State to accept safeguards, in accordance with the terms of the Agreement, on all source or special fissionable material in all peaceful nuclear activities within its territory, under its jurisdiction or carried out under its control anywhere, for the exclusive purpose of verifying that such material is not diverted to nuclear weapons or other nuclear explosive devices.... 7. The Agreement should provide that the State shall establish and maintain a system of accounting for and control of all nuclear material subject to safeguards under the Agreement, and that such safeguards shall be applied in such a manner as to enable the Agency [IAEA] to verify, in ascertaining there has been no diversion of nuclear material from peaceful uses to nuclear

weapons or other nuclear explosive devices, findings of the State's system. The Agency's verification shall include, *inter alia*, independent measurements and observations conducted by the Agency.

As noted by the United Nations,

The political objectives of NPT safeguards [administered by the IAEA] are to assure the international community that a [non-nuclear weapon] State party to the treaty is complying with its peaceful-use undertakings and to deter, through the risk of early detection, the diversion from peaceful uses or the misuse of nuclear material and facilities.[1]

The IAEA safeguards regime includes audits, surveillance cameras, inventory controls such as tags and seals (the latter categorized as "active," passive," or "intrinsic"), laboratory analysis, and on-site inspections. (In cooperation with the IAEA, the Euratom organization also administers safeguards.) As a tenet for banning nuclear weapons, safeguards must be extended to all countries, although in practice safeguards are only applicable to states possessing fissionable material.

The IAEA is obliged to provide "peaceful" nuclear assistance to NPT nonnuclear weapon states, because they have pledged in the NPT to nonpossession of nuclear weapons and acceptance of IAEA safeguards on fissionable material for peaceful use. Such use includes electricity from nuclear power plants, which also produce plutonium that is embedded in but separable from irradiated or "spent" reactor fuel. Given the dual, potentially contradictory mission of the IAEA to *assist* states in peaceful nuclear development and also administer safeguards, it is uncertain what role the IAEA could perform under a genuine nuclear weapons ban. The IAEA, however, does possess the long-time safeguards expertise, so many of its personnel inevitably would be of service to the worldwide verification regime of a nuclear weapons ban treaty.

The IAEA should not be dissolved, because it provides valuable assistance on such matters as reactor safety, nuclear medicine, and use of isotopes in agricultural studies. A smaller IAEA could continue such "peaceful assistance" to interested states, while the nuclear ban's technical secretariat would administer safeguard measures for the worldwide nuclear treaty—unencumbered by an IAEA-reminiscent requirement to also aid states' "peaceful" nuclear energy enterprises.

VERIFICATION ELEMENTS

A nuclear weapons ban will require great transparency of peaceful nuclear operations, plus revealed historical records of past warhead production and dismantling, as well as full reporting of all extant nuclear weapons. (At present, there is no such worldwide accountancy.[2]) Obviously, verification of actual warhead elimination will be more challenging than verification of closure or conversion of production facilities. For warheads, techniques such as perimeter portal monitoring of nuclear weapons dismantling sites will be important, as will tagging of warheads awaiting dismantling and utilization of their radiation "signature" to ascertain that real warheads slated for dismantling have not been replaced with spurious ones.[3] The treaty requirement of states' declarations of nuclear weapons, facilities, and material is consonant with Danish physicist Neils Bohr's words in a 1950 open letter to the United Nations:

> Real cooperation between nations on problems of common concern presupposes free access to all information of importance for their relation. Any argument for uphold-ing barriers of information, based on concern for national ideals or interest, must be weighed against the beneficial effects of common enlightenment and the relieved ten-sion resulting from such openness.[4]

Ronald Reagan's dictum, "Trust but verify," also presupposes ample informa-tion exchange—or else verification would be nugatory.

Fundamentally, the information and results of inspections would be public information. States would need to know the results of inspections, including data on which conclusions are based, to establish and maintain states' confi-dence in the treaty's operation. But if all states know such information, then the information could easily become public, and thus the "baseline inventories" and other information should be available to the world without the pretense of secrecy or restriction to just some states under the transparency and reporting requirements of the nuclear ban. To comply internally with this aspect of the treaty verification regime, today's nuclear weapon states in particular would need to revise their national laws on "classified information" (but with the rec-ompense of a nuclear weapons–free world).

The proposed nuclear ban treaty does not require that states "freeze" their arsenals in place during the weapons-elimination period, although inspectors would physically visit the sites of weapons, including submarines, to record baseline inventories with identification such as serial number and radiation sig-nature. The treaty give states a few years or so (see chapter 7) to eliminate all nuclear weapons, and if a state possessed only a relatively small arsenal, then it probably would be reluctant to freeze its weapons in place and thereby expose them to a potential arsenal-liquidating attack, especially a nuclear one— although as soon as a nuclear ban treaty enters into force (before states' decla-rations of warheads and nuclear material), states by treaty forswear the use of nuclear weapons.

What, then, would prevent a state from "cheating" on its declarations of warheads? With world attention on the unanimously joined treaty's incipient timetable for elimination of nuclear weapons, it is exceedingly improbable that a state would attempt to perpetrate a deception such as hiding and failing to declare warheads, or likewise for a stock of HEU or plutonium. The latter is conceivable because, especially for the United States and Russia, plutonium and HEU declarations will be verifiable only within an estimated 2 to 4 percent margin of error, which represents enough U.S. and Russian HEU and plutonium for many dozens of weapons. But despite the geopolitical force of the treaty's unanimity, let it be assumed that a deception by a state in its declarations *does* occur. Although such a deception *might* last some weeks or months without detection from the outside or a revelation from the inside, the evil-doing state would have no monopolistic nuclear hammer on others. Because the treaty's warhead-elimination period lasts three years at least, current nuclear powers would still possess some nuclear weapons during that period. Every passing day would represent a chance of exposure, and opposition to a treaty-violating state would be voiced by the entirety of the world's other states. A single citizen, worker-citizen, or defector who initiated exposure of a deception would bring a state and its leaders to grossest ignominy in the mind of humanity and give rise to fury across the globe. With such results being so unavoidably foreseeable, states would be loathe to embark on a course of treaty violation. And why would a state join the prospective nuclear ban in the first place if it intended to maintain nuclear weapons, which can be done so much more easily and "defensibly"—because some other states have them—in the absence of a worldwide nuclear ban?

Next, on the question of "managed access" during inspections, a feasible policy is formulated in Article 7(a) of the current IAEA "Model Additional Protocol" (IAEA INFCIRC/540), which stipulates that upon request by an NPT state, "arrangements" shall be made

> in order to prevent the dissemination of proliferation-sensitive information, to meet safety or physical protection requirements, or to protect proprietary or commercially sensitive information. Such arrangements shall not preclude the Agency from conducting activities necessary to provide credible assurance of the absence of undeclared nuclear material and activities at the location in question.

The apex of rigor in an acceptable inspection regime is "challenge inspection," which would be an element of the nuclear ban treaty. At the request of a state, a challenge inspection would be conducted by the technical secretariat of the treaty-created, overall "Organization for the Prohibition of Nuclear Weapons." Paralleling the current CWC (treaty), a state's challenge inspection request would be granted and carried out unless the request was determined to be abusive, frivolous, or clearly beyond the scope of the nuclear ban treaty by three-quarters vote of the nuclear ban's executive council.

It is by no means certain that challenge inspections would be undertaken or with any frequency even over centuries; states would be on their guard to comply with a unanimous ban, to avoid inciting alarm abroad. Also (and as would be foreseen by treaty parties), any state that presumptuously attempted to push through a challenge inspection request but offered no significant evidence of another state's wrongdoing would embarrass itself and invite acrimony from the range of treaty parties—for apparent attempted abuse of the treaty's challenge inspection provision.

With the 1997 inception of the welcome "Model [safeguards] Protocol Additional to the Agreements Between the States(s) and the International Atomic Energy Agency" (earlier-cited IAEA INFCIRC/540), the IAEA strengthened its capabilities and procedures for ascertaining that NPT non-nuclear weapon states are not concealing or diverting plutonium or enriched uranium. However, the bolstered IAEA measures such as environmental sampling ("high-performance trace analysis") at undeclared sites must be accepted by individual NPT states to legally apply to them and not all have acceded to the stricter inspection measures of IAEA INFCIRC/540. And again, no IAEA safeguards are required on fissionable material for the few states outside the NPT nor for the five NPT nuclear weapon states. In addition, neither today's NPT nor the IAEA Statute contains provision or authorization whereby an *individual NPT state party* can directly invoke a challenge inspection—unless turned down by three-quarters vote of an international body such as the IAEA board of governors or, with a new nuclear treaty, its executive council. Furthermore, if an NPT non-nuclear weapon state under today's NPT felt that the IAEA was acting too presumptuously in seeking out suspected nuclear activity through IAEA requests for "special inspections," the state could drop out of the NPT and thereby shed the NPT international legal obligation of nonpossession of nuclear weapons. ("Special inspections" refers to nonroutine verification visits or searches on initiative of a verification regime, whereas challenge inspections are prompted by individual states.)

Challenge inspections are the great democratizers of treaty verification, because any state party can avail itself of this "strongest" type of inspection. Under the proposed nuclear ban treaty, however, and paralleling today's chemical weapons treaty (the CWC), a challenge inspection request would be rejected if voted against by three-quarters of the nuclear ban's executive council. This raises the question of a state's legitimate response if its challenge inspection request was denied, but the state firmly believed another state was "materially breaching" the treaty. In this contingency, one can simply say that the former state would be justified in announcing its suspension (not termination) of treaty participation, if the suspension was based on reasonable and publicly articulated evidence of ongoing material breach. But an executive council denial of a challenge inspection request accompanied by evidence would be acutely improbable, particularly with all states being treaty parties and all having a stake in maintaining the benefits of a world without nuclear weapons.

U.N. Security Council Resolution 1441, adopted on November 8, 2002, imposed unprecedented strictness of inspection on Iraq. Comments follow on leading points of Iraqi inspection (December 2002–March 2003), with a focus on whether the measures would be appropriate for a nuclear ban treaty that must be acceptable to all states.

Iraq under Resolution 1441 was required to fully permit access for inter-views and to allow interviews outside of Iraq and facilitate travel of interview-ees and their families outside Iraq. The gravamen here is whether countries such as the United States, France, and Britain would agree to such a provision for worldwide nuclear ban inspection, and the answer is probably not, based on its breadth (in a forthright interpretation of "full access"). Nuclear ban inspec-tors could *request* an interview with anyone, however, and inspectors surely would report to the treaty's executive council a denial of an interview with a person who could shed light on a demonstrably suspicious situation. World pressure would immediately mount on any state pursuing such a path of trucu-lence, and this fairly can be deemed unlikely under a treaty that is unanimously joined and is nondiscriminatory in its provisions.

U.N. Resolution 1441 properly granted no authority to inspectors or the international community to "force" Iraqis to talk. Under worldwide prohibition of nuclear weapons, various currents of "societal verification" (see chapter 12) would enhance the likelihood of voluntary revelation from within the country about any treaty noncompliance.

Iraq under U.N. resolution 1441 had to provide inspectors full access anytime and anywhere, "including immediate, unimpeded, unconditional, and unob-structed access to presidential sites." If applied worldwide, these words evoke images of inspectors peering into White House quarters or burrowing their way into the U.S. Capitol or the Supreme Court. Legally, a search of such esteemed places (of any state) could transpire under nuclear ban treaty terms, as pursuant to a state's challenge inspection request (if not turned down by the three-quarters executive council vote). For banning nuclear weapons, it is apposite that no sites per se be off limits to inspectors, because a state "could" attempt to hide some-thing at a "presidential" or similar site. But assuming no evidence of wrongdoing was presented, the very request for such a challenge inspection would outrage the world and be turned down by the executive council.

Continuing, Iraq was mandated under Resolution 1441 to provide to inspec-tors the names of all present and past persons associated with biological, chemi-cal, nuclear, and missile programs and facilities. This stricture is probably a step too far for acquiescence by all states, and in any event, it would be a mas-sive and inexact undertaking, given the innumerable persons employed over the years in mass destruction weapons-related programs of various countries.

Also, inspectors in Iraq had the right to declare exclusion zones for freezing a site and its "surrounding areas and transit corridors," in which event Iraq was required to "suspend ground and aerial movement so that nothing is changed in or taken out of a site being inspected." This is a close call for a worldwide nu-clear ban, but it would be beneficial and only possibly would come into play in the unlikely contingency, under a unanimous treaty, that activity at a site was or had been evinced as seemingly in violation of the nuclear ban.

Finally, inspectors in Iraq under U.N. resolution 1441 had the right "at their sole discretion verifiably to remove, destroy, or render harmless all prohibited weapons, subsystems, components, records, materials, and other related items, and the right to impound or close any facilities or equipment for the production thereof," and to "seize and export" equipment, materials, and documents. Obviously, many states would object to this type of "inspection" provision, and it is unsuitable for a nuclear weapons ban applicable to all states.

Again, nuclear ban inspection cannot be identical to that imposed on Iraq and implemented for four months (until inspectors were pulled out for their safety just before the 2003 U.S.-led military action) by the IAEA, and for chem-bio weapons, the U.N. Monitoring, Verification, and Inspection Commission. But "challenge inspection" would be available to any state, and to quell abuse with rejection of a challenge request upon three-quarters vote of the treaty's executive council.

HEU TO LEU

Turning attention more closely now to fissionable material, which is the object of IAEA safeguards for NPT non-nuclear weapon parties, U.S. taxpayer-funded programs (Departments of Defense, Energy, and State) for "threat reduction" have achieved valuable progress in securing materials such as HEU and plutonium in Russia and other former Soviet territories. (The private Nuclear Threat Initiative has assisted in similar endeavors, including its provision of $5 million in 2002 to enable spiriting away from a poorly secured Yugoslav site a bomb-usable quantity of HEU.) The U.S. government programs include protection, control, and accountancy of nuclear material, consolidation of nuclear sites, U.S. acquisition for $12 billion over 20 years of 500 tons of Russian weapons HEU blended down to LEU (usable as reactor fuel), dismantling so far of more than 6,500 warheads and several hundred bombers and ballistic missiles, and alternative employment for nuclear scientists and technicians. The U.S. Congress in the early 1990s foresightedly ushered into reality the threat reduction initiatives, and they serve predominantly to decrease the possibility of "leakage" of nuclear material, weapons, or expertise from the former Soviet Union.[5] The United States is the largest provider of threat reduction funds, but other countries are also contributing, including Britain, Canada, France, Germany, Italy, and Japan. (Annual U.S. spending for threat reduction amounts to about $1.2 billion.)

LEU at enrichments close to but below the LEU-HEU demarcation (20 percent enrichment in readily fissionable isotope uranium-235) could be used to make a nuclear weapon; however, to do so would require about 850 pounds of 20 percent enriched HEU, and even more material if the LEU was at 18 or 19 percent enrichment. Furthermore, the 850 pounds required at the LEU-HEU demarcation assumes an "implosion" weapon, which would be beyond the resources and capacity of terrorists to fabricate. So, although a nearly half-ton mass of LEU at just below 20 percent enrichment could be used to make a single nuclear weapon, the terrorists' chance of success would be virtually nil because of the major amount of LEU required—which could not easily be smuggled out of a facility—and, more crucially, the necessity of very advanced technological resources to construct an implosion weapon. If a *state* decided to "break out" of the unanimously joined nuclear ban, the state would do so in the direct, efficient way: using stocks of plutonium (see overall discussion of plutonium later in this chapter). As little as 10 pounds of "weapons-grade" purity plutonium-239 is sufficient for a nuclear weapon (implosion), if its core is surrounded by an effective "tamper" (allowing supercriticality to occur with such a small amount of plutonium). Under the ban, however, all stocks of plutonium as well as enriched uranium would be under international safeguards to provide notice of any action by a state to divert or seize away material from inspectors' purview.

A general proposition for banning nuclear weapons is that states' stocks of HEU must be blended down to LEU, defined as less than 20 percent uranium-235 enrichment. Consequently, nuclear reactors using HEU fuel would need to cease doing so, according to treaty terms six months before the end of the weapons-elimination period. HEU reactors that a state wished to continue in operation would have to be converted to LEU fuel. But an obstacle looms here, because HEU fuel is used by a few leading countries for naval propulsion reactors. If HEU fuel *is* permitted under the nuclear ban treaty, then during an HEU-powered submarine's voyages, the HEU would be outside the treaty's safeguards regime and would have the imaginable consequence of being diverted and employed as a nuclear weapon's explosive core.

But are worldwide nuclear material safeguards *necessary*? Wouldn't the unanimity of the treaty, and its benefits to humanity, prevent any treaty breakout or redevelopment of nuclear weapons? Indeed, states would not break out—in part because they would readily foresee the massive negative reaction from re-exposing humanity to nuclear weapons. But a verification regime will enhance standards of control and accountancy of nuclear material thanks to the treaty's requirement of international safeguards and (see later in this chapter) physical protection of their material by individual states against diversion or theft. Verification will add a level of deterrence to cheating, even if it is unnecessary for maintaining the elimination of nuclear weapons under a treaty joined by all states before its entry into force. To date, unanimity has not been achieved in the history of treaties; but the climb to achieve nuclear ban unanimity seemingly would start from a high plateau of willingness to join, insofar as the great majority of states are already non-nuclear weapon parties to the NPT.

Let it be supposed for the moment that rather than a treaty-required blending down of all HEU to LEU, possession of *limited* stocks of HEU is permitted. Merely assuming a great reduction in HEU, the risk of a terrorist organization obtaining HEU would be curtailed. Great reduction also would remove from states any access to large quantities of weapons-usable HEU and would decrease the need for extensive commercial plutonium reprocessing. This need for reprocessing would decrease because of the availability, for several decades at least, of an ample supply of LEU (including stocks blended down from weapons-grade HEU) for the world's prevalent, light-water-moderated nuclear power reactors. Again, the problem with permitting naval or other marine reactors to use HEU fuel is that a vessel when away from port could dock at a secret location, whereupon the HEU fuel could be extracted from the reactor for HEU use as the explosive core of a nuclear weapon and would not need further, laborious uranium enrichment (although some processing of HEU-containing fuel elements would be necessary to use the HEU as bomb material).

An act such as the above by a state would brand it as an international outlaw and a traitor to humanity, the knowledge of which would act as a barrier to such an undertaking, particularly so under a treaty with the geopolitical force of unanimity. But if unsafeguarded HEU is permitted for the handful of states with HEU naval propulsion reactors, then to avoid an unacceptably "discriminatory" treaty, all states would likewise have to be permitted unsafeguarded possession of HEU, in which case safeguards on all fissionable material might as well be scrapped. This would probably be unacceptable to various countries, so the proposed treaty mandates cessation of HEU use effective six months before completion of weapons elimination (see chapter 7).

Ending HEU use would not compel those states with nuclear navies to revert to diesel propulsion (diesel-electric for submarines), but rather, to comply with the treaty's prohibition of HEU, the states could only use fuel of less than 20 percent enrichment (LEU), which is less efficient than HEU and requires more frequent refueling. Early U.S. naval reactor cores lasted only a few years, whereas the intended core life of the new *Virginia*-class attack submarine is equal to the 33-year design life of the vessel.

In addition to 9 nuclear-powered aircraft carriers, the United States has 74 nuclear submarines: 14 SSBNs or "boomers" carrying multiwarhead nuclear missiles (plus four SSBNs now armed with non-nuclear weapons), and 56 SSNs—attack subs, devoid of nuclear weapons. Smaller nuclear fleets are held by Russia, Britain, France, and China; Russia also operates seven nuclear-powered icebreakers and an "Arctic transport." U.S.-British naval reactor fuel is enriched to 95 percent or greater uranium-235, while enrichments for Russian reactors are believed to range from 12 to 90 percent, for French reactors from 7 to 90 percent, and for Chinese reactors just 3 to 5 percent. (Most Russian enrichments are toward the high end.)

Although there would be sacrifices in the core lifetime of HEU naval reactors upon conversion to LEU, and additional cost of more frequent refueling, the U.S. expense side would be more than offset by retirement from service of today's 14 huge, nuclear-armed ballistic missile submarines (the SSBNs). Even if the United States did not decommission several of its SSBNs to hedge against a (conceived) nuclear ban "breakout" (or to serve on non-nuclear weapons missions), most personnel, maintenance, and other costs would be obviated.

The U.S. Navy may initially oppose the prospect of converting naval reactors to less-efficient LEU fuel use. The gain, though, of conversion is enabling the worldwide elimination of nuclear weapons, so they will no longer threaten naval personnel, their families, fellow Americans, and persons worldwide. Countries with nuclear navies could not with probity claim of weapons-usable HEU that the nuclear ban treaty should allow them to have unmonitored possession of HEU as naval reactor fuel, whereas North Korea, Iran, and other countries should not possess HEU due to its unique usability by these states, or if acquired by terrorists, in a relatively "simple," gun-type weapon.

Over a period of at least a few years states with nuclear navies would convert their HEU reactors, beginning 60 days after unanimity of accession by states to the treaty as announced by the U.N. Secretary-General (and assuming no state's objection during those 60 days causes termination of that presumptive 180-day interval toward treaty entry into force). Four more months would then ensue, ending with entry into force, and thereafter a few months at least would pass while states enact satisfactory domestic implementing legislation (see chapter 10). Over the next several or more months, states' declarations of nuclear material, weapons, and facilities would be submitted and their verification would be undertaken by the nuclear ban technical secretariat (inspectorate). After this time, assuming that all states concur, the treaty process (30 days later) would begin the "next step" of weapons elimination. Positing the minimum elimination period as three years (see chapter 7), cessation of HEU use would occur at the end of the first 30 months. Adding projections of several months for enactment by states of appropriate implementing legislation, an additional few months for alterations by states of nuclear "classified information" laws, and more time for states' declarations and their verification to fellow states' satisfaction, the U.S. and other nuclear navies then would have at least a few years following treaty unanimity and subsequent entry into force to convert HEU reactors to LEU (for those vessels judged worthy to be kept in service with LEU fuel).

Purists may object that a loophole is opened by permitting LEU-fueled marine reactors, because even today for NPT non-nuclear weapon states all enriched uranium (not just HEU) must be IAEA safeguarded. But the main reason for this is that LEU fuel use in reactors creates plutonium, embedded in but separable from irradiated reactor fuel. Under the worldwide nuclear ban, all uranium-enrichment activity would be monitored, to ensure no 20 percent or greater enrichment, but states would be allowed use of less than 20 percent enriched (LEU) fuel in naval or other (icebreaker) marine reactors. Those states under the ban would be assenting to and undertaking the major step of converting their HEU propulsion reactors to LEU, and because all states must join the nuclear ban treaty before it enters into force, it is here proposed that marine vessels be permitted under the treaty to operate with LEU fuel (without the requirement of conversion to diesel or diesel-electric power).

Conceivably, though, a nuclear submarine crew could dock somewhere, unload irradiated LEU fuel from the ship's reactor, and then transfer the fuel to a secret processing site—unlawful under the treaty because undeclared—where plutonium in the fuel could be chemically separated out, further processed, and illicitly fabricated into the fissile core of a warhead. This scenario would be irrelevant if the handful of nations with nuclear navies switched to diesel; and if all did so, then none would have a "nuclear propulsion" advantage over the others. Notwithstanding, a few countries might decline to sign a nuclear ban treaty if it mandates no nuclear propulsion at all. The middle-of-the-road path of the proposed nuclear ban is that LEU fuel (below 20 percent enrichment) must be used.

To facilitate the termination of the nuclear threat to all people, it would be within the realm of nobly grounded reason for the U.S. and other nuclear navies to conclude, "We will not attempt to stand in the way of elimination of mass destruction weapons. We realize that a nuclear ban treaty must be nondiscriminatory and that weapons-usable HEU in reactors of vessels at sea cannot be safeguarded."

Any scheme by a "fanatic cabal" or a "crazed leader" to illicitly extract plutonium from a submarine's irradiated LEU fuel would run a risk of disregard by a submarine crew, insofar as the machinations obviously would be in violation of the unanimously joined nuclear ban. Elimination of weapons of mass destruction is at least as beneficial to military personnel as to others, and the voice of conscience of many military personnel would at least pose a significant possibility that some would balk at acting in a manner so obviously prejudicial to peace, contrary to treaty law (to which a treaty's parties bind themselves), and pernicious to their country with opposition and obloquy against a treaty violator predictably to pour forth from all other states.

Finally, and most important on this issue of the proposed "permissibility" under a nuclear weapons ban of LEU for naval propulsion reactors: only the five most-longstanding nuclear weapon states have a nuclear naval force, plus a nascent one for India. Even under the nuclear weapons ban, those six states could easily and expeditiously create a substantial number of weapons from current plutonium stocks or stocks from future dismantled weapons (see upcoming section, "Plutonium and Reprocessing"). If such a state was to break out of the unanimously joined treaty, the state would simply expel (or apprehend) inspectors and proceed with dastardly reintroduction of nuclear weapons. Going the diversion route of LEU from submarines would yield many fewer weapons (at most one per attack sub), take much more time (for plutonium separation and its further processing), and, crucially, carry a clear-cut risk of report to the nuclear ban regime by any "participant" during the baleful scheme's planning. These considerations support the position here that LEU fuel would not pose a security risk. Again, this is borne out by the consideration that any state—just six now—with the nuclear expertise for naval propulsion would have the capability, and almost certainly would have the material (plutonium from dismantled weapons), to "break out" of the treaty much more swiftly and definitely than going through the time-consuming actions, for meager result, of scheming to surreptitiously extract plutonium (which is only about 1 percent of irradiated reactor fuel) from a naval reactor to create a bomb.

Let it be clear that international (nuclear ban technical secretariat) verification and monitoring *would* cover the enrichment, fabrication, loading, and unloading of naval propulsion LEU fuel (and also would cover the dismantling of nuclear weapons and the storage and disposition of former military-use HEU and plutonium). If, to the contrary, uranium enrichment for and fabrication of LEU naval propulsion fuel was *outside* the prospective treaty's purview, then some other states would protest, saying,

> We won't sign this prospective treaty. We don't have a nuclear navy, and by treaty terms all our enrichment activities are restricted to LEU and must be monitored, so we could not create HEU, whereas for countries with nuclear navies the uranium-enrichment and fuel-fabrication process is outside ban scrutiny—so such a state could easily and secretly undertake a major, treaty-violating, *HEU* enrichment program. This is unfair and it is discriminatory against us and other states.

Other than marine propulsion, the primary non-weapons use for HEU is in research reactors. The prevalence of research and test reactors using HEU has steadily declined, in part due to development of high-density LEU fuels at locales such as the U.S. Argonne National Laboratory. With prospective abolition of nuclear weapons as a nuclear ban treaty is negotiated and finalized for signature by states, it is more than likely that world opinion will turn against the use of HEU fuel in research reactors. The nuclear ban would prohibit such use, even though a minority of research reactors may therefore need to shut down, that is, if current efforts to develop high-density LEU fuels for all such reactors fall short. Nevertheless, the proposed nuclear ban treaty does allow limited, monitored production of HEU for any highly protected research project(s) that might require HEU, if a request and proposal is approved by three-quarters vote of the nuclear ban's executive council, including votes of all pretreaty nuclear powers.

HEU today is also used in medical isotope production, but the private companies involved would not be at a competitive disadvantage to one another if all used less efficient LEU instead of HEU. Or, under the executive council's treaty prerogative (mentioned above) and with the assent of all pretreaty nuclear powers, upon request of isotope producers, the council may institute a program whereby international security forces and other controls would be implemented to render safe the production and use of HEU solely as needed (if need can be shown) for medical isotope production.

The nuclear ban treaty deadline for completion by states of blending down HEU (primarily from dismantled weapons and research or naval reactor fuel) to LEU may need to be set at a time beyond the end of the weapons-elimination period. When the treaty is drafted and introduced, the date at which the treaty will achieve unanimous accession and six months later enter into force will be unknown; and Russia and the United States, while able to dismantle their warheads according to the treaty's elimination timetable, may not be able to convert their HEU stocks to LEU within that time span.

The proposed treaty sets the HEU-to-LEU deadline at a certain number of years, ascertained by correlation of various durations with a treaty scale of plausibly remaining Russian and U.S. quantities of HEU when, under the enacted nuclear ban, verification (by the treaty regime's technical secretariat) of nuclear material and weapon declarations is completed. If a nuclear ban entered into force now, perhaps a decade or more would be necessary for Russia to blend down its HEU, whereas achievement of unanimous accession and entry into force in the future may be preceded by such an extent of reduction in Russian HEU that the HEU blending-down period would be closer to or within the three- to five-year duration (see chapter 7) of the warhead-elimination period.

Even with conversion of HEU stocks to LEU under the treaty, every last quantity cannot be isolated and blended down because substantial amounts of HEU, as well as plutonium, are contained in scraps, wastes, and residues from decades of warhead production. To obtain usable quantities of material from these scraps would require complex, extensive processing, however, and for nonpeaceful purposes such endeavors would be prohibited by the nuclear ban treaty—and be backed by the unprecedented geopolitical force of unanimity.

PLUTONIUM AND REPROCESSING

Although world stocks of HEU are decreasing, primarily through the U.S. purchase over 20 years of 500 tons of Russian HEU from weapons blended down to LEU, plutonium for its part is ever increasing, with up to 8,000 tons of nuclear power spent fuel being generated annually (containing about 70 tons of plutonium). Plutonium in typical commercial power reactor spent fuel is non-weapons grade, but if separated from spent fuel, it could be used for nuclear weapons, although with greater difficulty and hazard in processing and uncertainty of full performance in a detonation. This latter uncertainty could be overcome by the expertise of a longstanding nuclear weapon state, and in practice, states use safer, less radioactively "hot" weapons-grade plutonium of nearly pure plutonium-239.

With respect to "final disposal" of plutonium from dismantled weapons, even the option of immobilizing plutonium mixed with high-level waste in steel-encased molten-glass logs would not with certainty or permanence rid the world of potentially retrievable plutonium. Decay of the waste's virulent radioactivity eventually would make the waste more easily handled, and the plutonium could be extracted. (Another prospective disposition for stocks of separated plutonium is use as mixed-oxide plutonium-uranium fuel [MOX] in specially modified reactors.)

Should spent fuel reprocessing—that is, separation of plutonium and its fabrication into a component of new reactor fuel such as MOX—be permitted under the ban? Or should states be required to use nuclear fuel (LEU) solely on the "once-through" basis, which leaves any unfissioned uranium and plutonium—the latter produced during normal operation of the reactor—undisturbed in highly radioactive spent fuel and submerged in cooling ponds? Focusing on just one of the world's countries, Japan, it quite probably *could* reject reprocessing without jeopardizing the country's present-day energy security (due to sufficient world supply of fresh LEU fuel for reactors on the "once-through" basis). But Japan probably would balk at prohibition of reprocessing of spent power reactor fuel in a nuclear weapons ban treaty, on the grounds that current uranium stocks and accessibly mineable ore will not last forever. Japan may authentically need or believes it will need recourse to substantial reprocessing in the future. Not only Japan but also other energy-hungry countries, in addition to today's handful of civilian reprocessers (most extensively France), might establish or expand reprocessing to supply additional nuclear fuel for power reactors. Therefore, although today's world supply of uranium for LEU reactor fuel militates against reprocessing now and by most estimates for several decades at least, reprocessing should not be proscribed by the nuclear weapons ban—being that it would be a permanent treaty that does not permit withdrawal. Emphatically, though, the possible eventual move to wider reprocessing by some states is no reason to encourage, hasten, or subsidize it. And if (as may be widely wished), today's fission-generated energy from nuclear reactors ever comes to be supplanted by "clean-burning" fusion technology, then that would terminate any necessity to reprocess or even use today's reactor fuel, with its highly radioactive fission products and plutonium in spent fuel.

Research is in progress on nuclear reactor fuel and safety innovations such as smaller, "modular" reactors with fueled-for-life cores, and "recycle-in-place" systems designed to negate the need for standard "external" reprocessing, with its concomitant separation of plutonium for further fuel use (or possibly for weapons). Such developments, though, may have their own disadvantages; for example, more widely distributed modular reactors would present more targets for terrorist attack. Regarding reactor fuel, thorium-based fuel (with its promise of greatly reduced plutonium production) is by some accounts advancing toward technical fruition, but an approach under study for reprocessing to make fuel more "proliferation resistant"—by designedly maintaining a strong measure of the spent fuel's "protective" intense radioactivity—may prove uneconomical and may pose hazards to legitimate handlers. In any case, large-scale or "bulk" reprocessing (to extract plutonium for fabrication into new fuel) presents the possibility that an effort at diversion could garner a significant quantity of plutonium without timely detection. A major mitigating element to this risk would be enhanced "near-real-time accountancy" of material, but its technical and economic feasibility is still uncertain. Increased at-plant measurements and more accurate analysis of reprocessing waste streams are other areas under investigation.

Since shortly after World War II, international control or even ownership of nuclear energy facilities and fissionable material has been a deemed possibility. If a nuclear weapons ban is to reify this vision, then at a minimum its details as well as its seeming acceptability to states large and small must be clear beforehand, or else one or more states predictably would decline to join the treaty and it would not come into effect. In this text, the premise is that "absolute" international control and ownership of nuclear material and facilities will not be part of a nuclear weapons ban; but a major, nearly-complete degree of international "control" of nuclear activities already exists for NPT non-nuclear weapon states. Under NPT terms those states, which number all but nine, are not prohibited from building reactors or conducting uranium-enrichment or pluto-nium-separation activities (as for reactor fuel), but as NPT parties they are obliged to declare and submit to international safeguards any and all such fission-able, peaceful-use material. With a worldwide nuclear weapons ban, all states would be under a regime of material surveillance and accountancy as intrusive as today's augmented safeguards (IAEA INFCIRC/540), plus full-time inspectors at reactors, expanded camera coverage, and safeguards on "yellowcake" (uranium milling) operations and on nuclear material final-disposal sites would be needed.

States today could withdraw from the NPT and sever NPT-mandated safe-guards (as North Korea did in 2003), whereas the proposed nuclear treaty does not permit withdrawal, so no state with a shadow of legality or world support could terminate its participation in the treaty's verification regime (unless a ma-terial breach of the treaty by another state prompted a state or states to tempo-rarily terminate their treaty participation). But the concern remains that "bulk reprocessing" will become widespread, and that with established, economically viable technology, a bomb-usable quantity of plutonium could be incrementally diverted without timely detection.

Under a nuclear ban, any state in the throes of conducting such a plutonium-diversion scheme would face a formidable interior obstacle deriving from the psychological weight of worldwide renunciation of nuclear weapons, which would render as problematic the recruitment and placement, without one slip, of conspirators (technicians, "bribed inspectors") within an internationally safeguarded bulk-reprocessing facility. Although potential conspirators argu-ably could be threatened for nonacquiescence, a person in that position could simply "cooperate" but also inform the treaty regime by any means available of the conspiracy, with sufficient details for credibility. Plus, the planning phase of such devilry—in violation of the state's words on the unanimously joined treaty—would involve at least a cabal, opening the distinct possibility of an early report by a person of conscience of the state's intended perfidy. Further-more, although the nuclear ban technical secretariat's accountancy of plutonium at a reprocessing site would lack precision (primarily due to waste stream losses of accountable material), the verification efforts and monitoring of facilities would pose a substantial risk of exposure of a diversion scheme. Finally, and arguably most important as a deterrent, omnipresent would be the cold fact that opposition to a treaty-violating state would come from the entire world.

For today's plutonium stockpiles, the proposed nuclear weapons ban does not mandate final disposal, such as immobilization with vitrification and then geo-logic burial. Again, some number of the world's states almost certainly will insist on maintaining at least an option to "reprocess," which centers on plutonium separated from spent reactor fuel. Furthermore, it probably will take many years for Russia and the United States to complete final disposal of their currently declared excess plutonium, and longer still for the disposal of much greater quantities from dismantled weapons under the nuclear ban. In light of the indeterminate but massive expense involved, and with it the uncertainty and distantness of a viable completion deadline, the nuclear ban on this count too should not mandate final disposal. Instead, all stocks would be under safeguards administered by the technical secretariat of the nuclear ban treaty, and all states would be bound to fealty to the treaty by the geopolitical, legal, psychological, and moral force of voluntary, unanimous accession by states before entry into force.

If possession of safeguarded plutonium is not prohibited, why then does the nuclear ban treaty require HEU to be blended down to LEU? First, to increase LEU stocks and thereby decrease for as long as possible any unwise, premature, excessive support for plutonium reprocessing. Second, to slash to zero or virtually so the risk of terrorist nuclear creation *via* stolen, sold, or diverted nuclear material, because HEU (not plutonium) is the usable material for a relatively rudimentary, gun-type nuclear bomb. Third, to remove from both large and small states any access to stockpiles of readily weapons-usable HEU.

The likelihood of the ongoing existence of plutonium stocks (internationally safeguarded) would not vitiate the nuclear weapons ban. Undergirding the ban would be, first, the status of the treaty as joined by all states before entry into force or imposition of any obligations. Second, the benefits to all people and states of worldwide compliance with the treaty—that is, freedom from nuclear war, freedom from "false-alarm" nuclear strike, freedom from risk of terrorist bomb acquisition (from a state), and virtually eliminated risk of terrorist bomb creation as stocks of weapons-usable HEU are blended down to LEU. Third, the deterrent wall of the certainty of international outrage and deeper consequences if a state was ever discovered as violating any provision of the treaty, including required declarations of nuclear material and its submission to international safeguards. Fourth, the deterrent force of the prospect of whistle-blowing (see chapter 12) or exposure by the treaty inspection regime, if a state ever attempted to set in motion a plan to surreptitiously violate the unanimously signed, beneficial treaty.

Protection and Transport of Nuclear Material

International safeguards on nuclear material, the heart of a treaty verification regime, do not directly address the physical protection of material against the risks of theft by outsiders, or diversion from within, or "terrorist assault" on a repository. The IAEA's recommendations for physical protection of material are set forth in IAEA INFCIRC/225/Rev. 4, "The Physical Protection of Nuclear Material and Nuclear Facilities." The instrumentalities of this 28-page document, or any pretreaty sequel, are integrated into the proposed nuclear ban treaty, so they would no longer be optional for states to follow.

In general (but see "transport" exception below), and as is the case today, under the nuclear ban it would be individual states that have the responsibility for the protection of nuclear material—by required compliance with IAEA INFCIRC/225/Rev. 4. For the part of the nuclear ban technical secretariat, its inspectors would be unarmed and would not be charged with the impossible task of preventing a state from seizing plutonium from a storage, reprocessing, or fuel-fabrication site (in a treaty breakout scenario). By terms of the treaty, though, former nuclear weapon states would be authorized to have their own external surveillance teams at those locations (as well as HEU sites during its blending down) to maintain continuous video and audio transmission to their states' governments. This would provide immediate notice of any irregular, unanticipated entry to a site by state operatives, as for the removal of material for nuclear weapon use. If transmission was ever terminated, that too would alert other states that a breakout did or may have occurred.

The nuclear ban's "transport" exception to states' responsibility for the physical security of their material and facilities provides that, during transport, the shipment be accompanied and protected against terrorist assault by an internationally comprised (and possibly U.N.-affiliated) Nuclear Protective Force, which would be paid for as an expense of the treaty inspection regime. Such force could not stop a determined seizure by a *state* of plutonium in transmit, but the armed personnel would be in constant communication with designated authorities of the former nuclear weapon states (and perhaps others that may wish to be included). On the extremely remote chance that a state ever broke out of the treaty by commandeering its own material while in transit, an indication of trouble could be conveyed in the few seconds (at the very least) before takeover of the material, thereby apprising other states of the apparent material breach. And, if redundancy may be excused on this point: the chance of treaty breakout is miniscule at most, primarily due to the impact of unanimous, voluntary accession by states before treaty entry into force, the predictable certainty of intense worldwide opposition to a treaty violator, and the benefits to all people of a nuclear-free world.

Before but in conjunction with transport, accountancy and monitoring of any treaty-permitted peaceful removal of plutonium stocks from a state's site (such as for vitrification and geologic burial) would be under the eye of international inspectors as a matter of course. In addition, representatives of the permanent members of the nuclear ban's executive council would be accorded entrance to the site and would directly observe the process.

KEY POINTS

With appreciation to the reader for long attention to this chapter, key points are as follows. First, because HEU is the material for terrorist or state creation of a gun-type, relatively simple nuclear weapon, under the nuclear ban treaty, HEU stocks are blended down to LEU. A consequence is that today's research reactors using HEU must cease doing so, but with an exception for any highly protected HEU research projects approved by three-quarters vote of the executive council, including unanimous vote of permanent council members.

Second, naval and other (icebreaker) marine nuclear propulsion is permitted under the treaty, but only with less-efficient LEU fuel. If, instead, unsafeguarded HEU fuel for naval propulsion *were* permitted, then to avoid an unacceptably discriminatory treaty, states such as North Korea and Iran would also have to be permitted unsafeguarded possession of readily weapons-usable HEU, which likely would be unacceptable to various states.

Third, the nuclear ban treaty does not prohibit reprocessing of spent fuel, because only a finite supply of uranium exists for future use as LEU reactor fuel, and on that basis several or more states probably would not consent to surrender forever their option to reprocess.

Fourth, the treaty does not require that world stocks of separated plutonium, including from dismantled weapons, undergo final disposal such as vitrification with ground-up high-level nuclear waste and then underground storage. If tentative steps are indicative, final disposal would require so great an expense and effort that Russia and the United States may not be able to ensure that they could achieve this by a reasonably set future date. Also, assuming reprocessing is ongoing to any extent, stocks of separated plutonium would still exist (as a component for fabrication of new fuel such as MOX); however, plutonium would be under international safeguards administered by the nuclear ban technical secretariat, the transport of stocks would be under guard and escort of the international Nuclear Protective Force, and pretreaty nuclear weapon states would be entitled to their own observation posts at plutonium storage, reprocessing, and fuel-fabrication sites.

Fifth, physical protection of nuclear material is prescribed for states by treaty mandate that states comply with IAEA recommendations as embodied in INFCIRC/225/Rev. 4 (or any pretreaty sequel).

Sixth, states agree by treaty to application of systematic (routine) inspections, special inspections on initiative of the treaty verification regime, and challenge inspections at the behest of individual states—with the latter carried out unless turned down by three-quarters vote of the treaty's executive council as being frivolous, abusive, or clearly beyond the scope of the treaty.

Would problematic states such as NPT-dropout North Korea join a nuclear ban? And would non-NPT states India, Pakistan, and Israel join?

6

Problematic States

First considering North Korea, that country in 1994 signed the U.S.-North Korea "Agreed Framework." The Framework obliged North Korea to freeze most operations and projects of its nuclear program, including de-activation of a small, 5 megawatt graphite-moderated reactor (capable of using unenriched or "natural" uranium as plutonium-producing reactor fuel), in exchange for the construction (subsidized primarily by South Korea and Japan) of two large, modern, light-water-moderated reactors safeguarded by the International Atomic Energy Agency.[1] The United States also consented to arrange for a supply of fuel oil to North Korea at an annual U.S. taxpayer cost of about $100 million.

The Clinton-era 1994 Framework did admirably bring a halt to plutonium-based growth of the North Korea nuclear program, with the freeze of nuclear facilities. Also, 8,000 previously irradiated fuel rods were "canned" and placed under IAEA safeguards, thereby becoming unavailable for separation of plutonium and its fabrication into the fissile cores of an estimated four to six weapons. In October 2002, as power reactor site work finally commenced in North Korea under the Agreed Framework, the United States accused North Korea of secretly pursuing uranium-enrichment capability, which a North Korean official admitted at the time,[2] precipitating the de facto demise of the Framework.

In part, the Framework's end limns the difficulty of eliminating nuclear weapons from certain states, when others retain theirs and do not intimate a willingness to eliminate their arsenals (if all states do likewise). Also, North Korea had its reasons, notably three, to complain that all along the United States was not fully living up to terms of the Framework. First, and as an understandable irritant to North Korea, the estimated six-year duration of the power reactor project did not start until the latter half of 2002, whereas the Framework had a completion target date for the first reactor of 2003 (so the basic schedule already was running five years late). Second, from the North Korean viewpoint the United States, up to the Framework's collapse in autumn 2002, had done little—particularly post-Clinton era—to advance toward the upgraded political relations and reduction of trade and investment barriers bespoken in Article II of the Framework. Third, the United States did not take action on the Article III(1) commitment that "The U.S. will provide formal assurances to the DPRK [North Korea], against the threat or use of nuclear weapons by the U.S." (In 2005 the United States did proclaim that it has "no intention" of attacking North Korea, but "no intention" is not a pledge; the U.S. reluctance to provide "formal assurance" or pledge against a U.S. nuclear attack is perhaps because other states would demand or ask for the same, and according such to North Korea or other states would vitiate the U.S. rationale for keeping nuclear weapons.) The United States is now faced with an archetypal dilemma of a world in which nuclear weapons have not been abolished. To what extent should the United States provide benefits and perhaps even sensible "concessions" to a country, without the stark appearance of succumbing to nuclear proliferation and "blackmail"? However, North Korea will not surrender its nuclear arsenal without substantial benefits—which in all likelihood otherwise would not be extended by the United States and others to a dictatorship. Furthermore, when and if the "denuclearization" of North Korea is consummated (including dismantling of its current, presumably small arsenal), the geopolitical force of a nonwithdrawal, *worldwide* nuclear ban treaty will be lacking.

In response to North Korea's seeming and surreptitious pursuit of uranium-enrichment technology, future oil deliveries by the United States under the Agreed Framework were terminated in November 2002, an action denounced by North Korea as a "wanton violation" of the Framework by the United States. In December 2002, following an IAEA call for cessation of North Korean concealment (and acceleration) of its nuclear weapons program, North Korea said that the United States should be faulted for destroying the Framework by casting North Korea as part of an "axis of evil" and that a nuclear weapons program was needed because the United States might be contemplating a preemptive strike. In December 2002, North Korea proclaimed its intention to reactivate its 5 megawatt reactor, followed two weeks later by North Korea's removal of IAEA camera surveillance of the 8,000 plutonium-bearing spent fuel rods. On January 10, 2003, North Korea declared its withdrawal from the NPT, and shortly thereafter IAEA inspectors were told to leave. At Beijing talks with the United States and China in April 2003, North Korea averred that it already had nuclear weapons capability; this claim was eventually validated by a small-yield, plutonium-fueled nuclear weapon test on October 9, 2006.

In May 2003 North Korea nullified its 1992 pact with South Korea for denuclearization of the Korean Peninsula, and in August 2003, unfruitful six-party talks were held at Beijing with participation of the United States, North Korea, South Korea, China, Russia, and Japan. On October 2, 2003, North Korea declared that it was using plutonium separated from the 8,000 fuel rods to fabricate nuclear weapons for the purpose of deterrence. The short-lived round of talks commencing on July 13, 2005, saw North Korea indicating that its return to deliberations (after a 13-month refusal) was due to a somewhat more "respectful" attitude then evidenced by the U.S. administration.

Even if a North Korean official had not reportedly admitted—although North Korea later disavowed it—to the pursuit of uranium-enrichment technology, the 1994 Agreed Framework was headed to a thorny area because of a requirement in Article IV(3). This article stipulated that, before delivery of key components for the two planned power reactors, North Korea must take "all steps that may be deemed necessary by the IAEA, following consultations with the Agency, with regard to verifying the accuracy and completeness of the DPRK's initial [1992] report on all nuclear material in the DPRK." The United States and some other countries believe that North Korea, before 1992, secretly separated one to three bombs' worth of weapons-grade plutonium from irradiated reactor fuel. If North Korea had ultimately come to comply with the above stricture of the 1994 Agreed Framework, then the IAEA's investigation (including nuclear archeology) presumably would have exposed North Korea's deceptive failure to declare the separated material in the country's initial, still-standing report on nuclear material to the IAEA. Official IAEA revelation of such deception would have resulted in world anger, as well as refusal to complete the new power reactors until the separated plutonium was accounted for, safeguarded, and possibly removed from North Korea. So, even if that country had not been clandestinely pursuing uranium-enrichment technology during some period at least when the plutonium-centered Agreed Framework held sway, a large obstacle was eventually to be encountered in the necessity of fully allowing IAEA verification activities before completion of the reactors, because North Korea would know that permitting such access would confirm to the IAEA (and to the world) North Korea's widely suspected, unreported prior separation of plutonium.

If, however, a *worldwide* nuclear ban were coming into effect, the incentive toward fullness of North Korea's and all states' compliance would be great, because the ban would be nondiscriminatory by barring nuclear weapons to all. In addition, the ban would benefit states by freeing them from fear of nuclear annihilation (which North Korea has claimed could be perpetrated by the United States). Furthermore, North Korea or any other state would unavoidably foresee that failure to provide satisfactory declarations or to permit necessary on-site verification visits and scrutiny under the unanimously joined treaty would invite bitter world condemnation and related consequences. (Under the proposed nuclear ban, the actual weapons-elimination period does not begin until after states vote by consensus—or at least "without demurral"—that the treaty process should "proceed to the next step," with such a vote being indicative of satisfactory compliance by all states with required declarations and cooperation in their baseline verification.)

On September 19, 2005, a Joint Statement of Principles (see appendix D) was issued from the resumed six-party talks in China. North Korea agreed to abandon "all nuclear weapons and existing nuclear programs" and to return "at an early date" to the NPT and IAEA safeguards. "Energy assistance" was to be provided to North Korea, and the six parties "agreed to discuss, at an appropriate time, the subject of provision of a [large, modern] light-water reactor" to North Korea (this being redolent of the now dead-letter 1994 Agreed Framework, with its intended provision of two such power reactors). The United States affirmed that it "has no intention to attack or invade" North Korea, and all parties averred that they would respect "sovereignty."

The cooperative spirit of the 2005 Statement of Principles soon dissipated, sparked by U.S. banking sanctions against North Korea for alleged international financial crimes. After much back and forth on this issue, and some U.S. concessions, in February 2007 North Korea agreed to freeze its nuclear facilities in exchange for fuel oil and to take further steps as more oil and other aid was proffered. Then in June 2008 North Korea took a significant step as it finished the promised inactivation of its 5 megawatt reactor; but many details for true denuclearization remain unsettled, including verification procedures for past plutonium production, sequencing of benefits to North Korea as it takes further steps, declaration of its current arsenal, and liquidation of those weapons.

As discussed in chapter 4, if there ever was a material breach of the proposed worldwide treaty, other states could temporarily ignore the treaty without violating the Vienna Convention on the Law of Treaties. This prerogative of response is counterpoised, however, by the nuclear ban treaty requirement that a state must publicly name, before undertaking an otherwise treaty-prohibited activity, the state that is in material breach and also announce when the breach is held to be rectified (if a state was ever grossly dilatory in acknowledging the manifest termination of a material breach, it would face international recrimination on a scale mirroring the geopolitical force of the unanimous treaty).

Next, regarding Iran—and assuming credence is given to suspicions by some observers that Iran currently desires to attain nuclear weapons—why expect accession to, and compliance with, a nuclear ban treaty by such a state as its government is presently constituted? First, because worldwide prohibition of nuclear weapons benefits Iran (and all states) by freeing Iran from possible attack by another's nuclear arsenal. Second, because all states, including current nuclear powers Israel, the United States, Britain, and France would be parties to the enacted ban, Iran would have no basis for thinking that "other countries have nuclear weapons but we do not, so we will by all means strive to attain them." Third, Iran would foresee that violation of a *worldwide* nuclear ban treaty would incite monumental opposition and related consequences from all compass points.

What, then, would ensue under the nuclear ban treaty *if* a state at some time failed to cooperate with inspectors or refused cooperation with another state's challenge inspection request duly authorized by the nuclear ban's executive council? First, the world at large would unite in opposition and take measures to cut off the renegade state from beneficial interactions. Second, the U.N. Security Council would meet under its Charter authority to deal with threats to the peace. Third, the U.N. Security Council, or possibly states acting individually, might initiate military action. Fourth, if the standoff was not promptly resolved, a few or several countries would temporarily recreate arsenals of nuclear weapons (very likely these would be relatively small scale). Fifth, the treaty-defaulting state would not soon be forgiven. With such consequences being eminently predictable, the world's states would have weighty incentives to abide by the nuclear ban.

Of all states, Israel is perhaps the most difficult to bring into a treaty banning nuclear weapons.[3] Israel's longtime policy has been to avoid discussing its possession of nuclear weapons, but there is uniform agreement that Israel has a modern arsenal, most likely in the range of 75 to 300 weapons. This is a thorn in the side to some of Israel's neighbors; but Israel never joined the 1968 NPT, so at least Israel is not forsworn in its nuclear possession—as is also true for non-NPT members Pakistan and India, as well as the five NPT nuclear weapon states (and North Korea did have the legal right to withdraw, as does any NPT party providing three months' notice and a statement of treaty subject-related "extraordinary events"). The status today of all but nine countries as NPT non-nuclear weapon parties is emblematic of the NPT's historical importance in stemming proliferation; but the treaty's atavisms, such as its five nuclear weapon states, and its lack of phased reductions or a deadline for the elimination of nuclear weapons, renders replacement of the NPT in the interests of "all living beings."

A treaty banning nuclear weapons must be voluntarily signed and ratified by all states before entry into force, so it would be Israel's choice whether it joins and therefore whether such a ban is enacted (assuming all other states joined). If Israel was a "lone holdout," other states could be expected to seek in various ways to encourage Israel to join, while allaying any security concerns within the states' individual or collective power. The decision to join must be up to each of the world's sovereign states, including Israel. It would be unfeasible to attempt to impose from outside a nuclear weapons ban on states, lest the ban's implementation necessitate full-scale military invasion and occupation. Furthermore, the nuclear ban treaty will embody significantly less moral and geopolitical force than if it takes effect only after all states voluntarily join, but with the important caveat that this voluntary abjuration of nuclear weapons does not apply to "new" or emergent states that may appear after the ban is in effect (based on the unlimited duration of the treaty and its proclamation that the prohibition of nuclear weapons development and possession is applicable everywhere once the treaty is joined by "all states" and enters into force).

In today's *absence* of a nuclear weapons ban, Israel's possession of a nuclear arsenal is at least as understandable as any state's. The countervailing and supreme security advantage to Israel of a worldwide ban is that it would *cut off to putative foes of Israel the path of nuclear weapons development and possession*, under the auspices of international inspection and with the geopolitical weight of a unanimously joined, nonwithdrawal treaty. Of at least equal benefit would be the virtually eliminated risk of nuclear terrorism against Israel, with worldwide safeguards plus standards of physical protection on fissionable materials, blending down of HEU to LEU, and dismantling of extant nuclear weapons (this latter erasing any vulnerability of weapons to theft by or diversion to terrorists).[4]

For various reasons, the security of Israel is a top priority of the United States. As declared by President George W. Bush, "In the event of an attack on Israel, the United States will come to the aid of Israel."[5] Nonetheless, upon commencement of multilateral negotiations for banning nuclear weapons, Israel may greet the effort coolly. This should not be surprising, insofar as no country can be expected to commit itself to any treaty until it is in final form. But assuming Israel decided to *join* the nuclear ban treaty, then Israel would be a benefactor to humanity, because Israel's accession (along with that of all other states) is required before the treaty enters into force or imposes any obligations.

To crystallize various benefits—which also apply to the other nuclear powers—Israel by joining would (1) cast off the spiritual burden of possessing nuclear weapons; (2) relinquish the possibility of using the ultimate "weapons of mass destruction" against fellow human beings; (3) no longer face today's threat of nuclear terrorism, with international safeguards and physical protection standards on fissionable material, blending down of HEU to LEU, and dismantling of current warheads; (4) free itself from potential vulnerability to another state's future nuclear weapons; and (5) drastically diminish its risk of being attacked by chemical or biological weapons (see chapter 9).

Considering next India and Pakistan, both in May 1998 became "declared" nuclear weapon states. As discussed in chapter 3, Pakistan will not join the current NPT and thereby renounce nuclear weapons unless India does, but India most probably will not join because, as India's cherished criticism has it, the NPT unjustly "discriminates" by its nonprohibition of nuclear weapons to the five most-longstanding powers (including India's neighbor China). The proposed nuclear weapons ban treaty resolves concerns of unfairness and discrimination, for all states renounce nuclear weapons and all nuclear possessors are subject to the treaty's weapons-elimination timetable (see chapter 7).

Conceivably, Pakistan may come to assert that it will retain nuclear weapons until tensions resolving Kashmir are resolved or greatly reduced. If Pakistan should take this position, existence of the prospective ban will bring a stronger world focus on Kashmir and concerted efforts to resolve its tensions. But even if Kashmir persists as unresolved (or merely becomes less tragically rent), Pakistan might well join a nuclear weapons ban that enters into force only after India and all states join—and Pakistan should, if it is to square itself with its steady presentment that it has not renounced nuclear weapons because India has not. For example, as reported by the Associated Press, Pakistan's Foreign Ministry spokesperson Aziz Ahmed Khan stated on May 5, 2003, "As far as Pakistan is concerned, if India is ready to denuclearize, we would be happy to denuclearize. But it will have to be mutual." Pakistan, like every country, would be freed from the threat of nuclear devastation under worldwide elimination of nuclear weapons; and India presumably would not reject a nuclear ban treaty that requires accession by China, Pakistan, and all other countries before entry into force.

Finally, with regard to Russia, the "opposing" West was never, even during the most frigid depths of the Cold War, intent on attacking Russia, and Russia now has no basis for believing that the West will ever launch a monstrous assault and attempt to conquer Russia. Russia at present undeniably could destroy West European and U.S. society in an hour with nuclear weapons, and this terrible capability will no longer exist under the elimination of these weapons. But is this a *deprivation* in a world in which all states have renounced and dismantled their nuclear weapons? The Russian people, who lost millions of civilians and soldiers in World War II, in all likelihood will perceive and embrace the mutual and profound benefit of a unanimously joined nuclear weapons ban. Russian receptivity to nuclear weapons elimination may have been augured at the June–July 2000 triennial U.N. Disarmament Commission conference, where—

> Among nuclear weapon States, the Russian Federation made the strongest pitch for nuclear disarmament, calling on all nuclear weapon States to launch a "comprehensive, forward-based, phased program, without artificial delays or other tactics." … It was [deemed by Russia] "timely and useful" to begin negotiations on nuclear disarmament using a concrete time frame.[6]

The next chapter delves into a structure of reductions culminating in worldwide elimination of nuclear weapons. An assumption is that when a ban enters into force, U.S. and Russian nuclear arsenals (total strategic and tactical warheads and bombs, including reserves and those to be dismantled) will still be much larger than those of the other nuclear weapon states. Another premise is that, before introduction for states' signatures of a nuclear ban treaty, Russia's total warhead count will be at the 15,000 level or below (most current estimates are 11,000–16,000). Since 1985 Russia has dismantled probably more than 20,000 warheads, and seemingly destined to spur further cuts are (1) the reasonably presumed status of most remaining Russian tactical warheads as nondeployed; (2) removal by the end of 2012 of 3,000-plus strategic warheads from delivery systems (under the Bush-Putin 2002 Moscow Treaty); and (3) in-progress acquisition by the United States of Russian LEU blended down from HEU from weapons being dismantled.

7

Weapons Elimination

By terms of the nuclear ban treaty, reductions leading to elimination of nuclear warheads only begin after specific conditions are met, as follows. Initially, all states formally join the treaty and it enters into force six months later (unless delayed by a state's objection, as discussed in chapter 3). Second, states enact their domestic (national) treaty implementing legislation, and these enactments are accepted "without demurral" by fellow members, that is, all states, of the treaty-created international "Organization for the Prohibition of Nuclear Weapons" (this terminology and the basic treaty regime structure are derived from the groundbreaking 1993 CWC; mirroring the CWC, the overall nuclear ban organization is composed of a conference of all parties, an executive council, and a technical secretariat). Third, states submit their declarations of nuclear material, facilities, and weapons. Fourth, the nuclear ban technical secretariat completes verification of declarations and reports on its findings. Fifth, states vote without demurral that treaty implementation should proceed to the next step of weapons elimination, with this vote representing a judgment on whether (or not) all states have complied with the treaty obligations of good-faith, detailed declarations, and cooperation in their baseline verification. (A single negative vote here by any state would delay commencement of weapons elimination until rectification of the declarations or verification-cooperation problem, and then again would require states without demurral to vote that treaty implementation continue.)

When the unanimously joined nuclear ban treaty enters into force, the date of commencement of the weapons elimination period will not be known, because it occurs 30 days after fulfillment of the above obligations.

"Weapons elimination" above denotes "warhead elimination." The terms are used in this book largely interchangeably, and the term "warhead" includes free-standing or "gravity bombs" as well as missile payloads. Even if all long-range nuclear-tipped missiles are dismantled, civilian space vehicles, ships, trucks, and some regular bombers could deliver nuclear weapons; so the key is elimination of warheads, backed by their worldwide prohibition.

For the proposed nuclear ban, the duration of the weapons-elimination period is set by treaty-specified correlation of enumerated, possible durations with a range of plausibly remaining quantities of U.S.-Russian nuclear warheads at the time (pursuant to declarations and their verification) when states vote without demurral that the treaty process should proceed to the next step of weapons elimination. The higher the number of U.S. or Russian warhead possession determines the length of the weapons-elimination period; and if for example Russia then has 9,000 warheads, including tactical, spares, and reserves, and the United States has only 5,000 warheads, treaty-mandated U.S. dismantling of warheads does not begin until Russia reduces to 5,000 (or *vice versa*) under the elimination timetable.

The touchstone in the treaty is the number of warheads and bombs (including both as "warheads" or "weapons"), without complicating distinctions such as size and deployment status. Warheads are counted as simply warheads whether they are large or small, in reserve, or awaiting dismantling. Under the ban each nuclear weapon state can decide which warheads it dismantles in meeting successive deadlines of the treaty's elimination period.

The treaty lists three possible elimination periods (three, four, or five years), with the actual length contingent on the greater quantity of U.S. or Russian warheads. The three-year elimination period would be applicable if a maximum of 7,000 warheads are in U.S. or Russian hands, the four-year period would apply if 7,000–10,000 are in their hands, and the five-year period would apply (although this scenario is unlikely) if more than 10,000 are in their hands. (The current U.S. total of roughly 7,000, about half of which is nondeployed or in reserve, is headed lower under current Pentagon plans and is down from a Cold War peak of some 32,000; the Soviet apex of about 40,000 warheads in 1986 is now down to an estimated 11,000–16,000, and with a majority of these nondeployed and some presumably awaiting dismantling.)

Entering the final phase of reductions, such as 12 months and up to 500 warheads, the treaty's progressively lower permissible ceilings on warhead possession by states are applicable to those possessing enough warheads to need to comply with each successive ceiling. During those final 12 months, the ceilings are delineated in the treaty on a month-by-month basis and then on a week-by-week basis, with a final day by which all warheads must be destroyed. (For U.S.-Russian reductions leading down to 500 warheads, the deadlines for ceilings are on a six- or three-month basis.)

Should the other nuclear powers be permitted to just "stand by" while Russia and the United States are eliminating thousands of warheads to reach the much lower, under-500 levels of the world's other nuclear possessors? This may be displeasing or even unacceptable to the United States and Russia; and therefore all countries possessing nuclear weapons, except the United States and Russia, are required within the first three months of the treaty's elimination period to dismantle a significant proportion of their warheads (such as 25 percent). If Pakistan then possesses 48 warheads, Pakistan would dismantle 12;

assuming Britain's current estimated arsenal size stays as is, Britain would reduce its arsenal by about 50 warheads.

The above is a compromise. Countries such as Britain, France, and China by all odds would want the United States and Russia to reduce their warheads to the former states' levels before those states commence reductions, whereas the United States and Russia presumably would prefer the other countries to reduce their arsenals proportionately from the start to U.S.-Russian reductions. But since both camps would be somewhat dissatisfied as well as somewhat satisfied with the approach here, feasibility may be indicated. The problem with proportionate reductions is that, for example, after 90 percent reduction the United States would have 500 warheads if it started with 5,000, whereas China starting with, say, 200 warheads would have only 20. This probably would not be acceptable to China, nor to France and Britain with their similar range of disparities.

When all states' arsenals are down to a maximum of perhaps 20 warheads, these would be dismantled within a span of four weeks. Warhead dismantling is under international monitoring throughout the elimination period, and all states would be under their prime, mutual avowal in the nuclear ban not to employ nuclear weapons.

Under the above schema, if Pakistan starts with 48 warheads and reduces by 25 percent within three months, it may then (if it wishes) retain its remaining 36 warheads until nearly the end of the elimination period. Since Pakistan's starting point is small compared with that of the five most-longstanding nuclear powers (especially the United States and Russia), it would be unfair to require Pakistan to dismantle warheads beyond an initial 25 percent reduction in advance of U.S.-Russian declines to the much lower levels of the other states.

Assuming Israel has 160 warheads at the time the nuclear ban enters into force, then Israel like all nuclear possessors except the United States and Russia also must dismantle 25 percent within the first three months of the elimination period. Thereafter Israel could retain its remaining warheads until all larger-scale nuclear possessors, following the treaty's timetable of phased reductions, have brought their arsenals down to Israel's new level of 120. All those countries along with Israel must then meet successive deadlines, monthly or weekly at this point, for ceilings on the decreasing permissible number of warheads.

Some States might, in response to the prospective treaty's requirement of a prompt 25 percent warhead decrease, build up their stockpiles so that the one-quarter reductions do not bring them below their pretreaty levels. This *is possible* but would not be a cost-free path; states would be aware that news of a significant increase likely would leak out and that the world would look askance at a state for increasing its warhead level (seemingly in anticipation of entry into force of the prospective worldwide nuclear ban). Furthermore, with prospective worldwide abolition of nuclear weapons on the immediate horizon, states might conclude that any increase in arsenals is just not needed.

But even though a pretreaty jump of 25 percent in arsenal size by a state or states would liquidate the essence of the "concession" to the United States and

Russia of having other nuclear states undertake a rapid, three-month, 25 percent reduction in arsenals, those latter states still would have to undertake the swift and transparent reduction of *disproportionately more* of their weapons (albeit from a raised level such as 25 percent) than required under the first three months of the elimination period for the United States and Russia. In addition, the United States and Russia would still, as at present, be possessors of substantially the greatest numbers of nuclear weapons throughout most of the elimination period. However, a nuclear arsenal increase (such as 25 percent) before the nuclear ban treaty entry into force cannot be *prohibited*, because under today's NPT-centered regime, the non-NPT states (Israel, India, Pakistan, and North Korea) and the five NPT nuclear weapon states are not barred by treaty from increasing their arsenals as they see fit. For the United States and Russia, however, the 2002 Moscow Treaty does mandate reduction by each to a maximum of 2,200 *deployed* strategic warheads at the end of 2012.

What if, during the weapons elimination period, a state suddenly stopped complying with its time-bound obligation to progressively dismantle nuclear warheads? This scenario strains credibility, given the geopolitical force of a unanimously joined treaty, but to alleviate concerns, the treaty stipulates that the time-bound progress of required warhead reductions is to be suspended, pursuant to one-quarter vote of the nuclear ban's executive council, if any treaty party by such vote is held to be in noncompliance. In this contingency, and with the elimination timetable suspended, states would be under no treaty obligation to continue dismantling warheads until the situation was accepted as rectified by vote without demurral of the executive council; and 30 days later the timetable for reductions leading to zero would resume.

Today's nuclear weapon states may object to "depending" on even a mere one-quarter executive council vote in the case of a state defaulting on the important weapons-elimination timetable. Disregarding this liberally set timetable would amount to a material breach of the treaty, however, so the United States or other countries would be entitled under Article 60(2)b of the Vienna Convention on the Law of Treaties (see chapter 4) to temporarily ignore the treaty and suspend ongoing dismantling of warheads (but recall the restriction in the proposed nuclear ban treaty that a state, before disregarding the treaty, must publicly name the other state that is held to be in material breach and, to avoid world castigation, would need to reveal sufficient evidence to credit the charge). The additional prospect of a treaty executive council–mandated suspension of warhead reduction provides further incentive for states to commit themselves to compliance with the timetable's elimination requirements.

Would states under the enacted treaty be permitted to *replace* or *refurbish* warheads? Refurbishment should not be prohibited, in acquiescence to the possibility (remote as it is) that a lengthy delay might interrupt treaty implementation—if, as just mentioned, a delay occurred during the weapons-elimination period or prior to that with respect to states' compliance with initial declarations and cooperation in their verification. However, after treaty-required declarations have been submitted by all states, any *replacement* of warheads (due to some apprehension of obsolescence, although nuclear weapons last for decades) would have to be fully reported to the nuclear ban's executive council and could not result in an increase in explosive yield.

A final point is that deformation of the perfectly machined plutonium cores for dismantled weapons is an obvious measure to prevent immediate reuse of the material for weapons and to physically and psychologically "finalize" the dismantling of warheads. Some states presumably would still possess internationally safeguarded plutonium stockpiles (see chapter 5), but these states would not have any bomb-ready plutonium "pits" (cores). These states also would not have any completed nuclear weapons that could be acquired by terrorists by theft or other means, and treaty-required blending down of HEU to LEU would virtually eliminate the chance of terrorist fabrication of a bomb.

8

Superseding Today's Non-Proliferation Treaty

One possible avenue for replacing today's inadequate NPT with a worldwide nuclear weapons ban is the "dropout" route, which hinges on some NPT non-nuclear weapon states causing global consternation by withdrawing from the NPT. A mass dropout, or even any number, would be alarming in its blow to the general, NPT-centered consensus against the spread of nuclear weapons; the NPT is generally considered "successful" only because the great majority of states have joined and therefore renounced possession of nuclear weapons— this as long as the states do not withdraw, and notwithstanding the five NPT nuclear weapon states. Under the dropout scenario, the ostensible objection of states in withdrawing from the NPT would not be development and wide proliferation of nuclear weapons but rather real trepidation of such proliferation, which would add urgency to calls for elimination of all nuclear arsenals.

The United States and other countries would try mightily to dissuade NPT parties from dropping out, such as promising energy assistance to North Korea when it came close to withdrawal in 1993 (resulting in the 1994 Agreed Framework, which collapsed eight years later). If various states do withdraw from the NPT, then their present or future fissionable material will no longer be required by the NPT to be safeguarded by the IAEA, and the states, being sovereign, could undertake concerted pursuit of nuclear weapons. (For the dozens of NPT states that are members of today's "regional nuclear weapon-free zone" pacts, eliminating the specific legal barriers to nuclear weapons development and possession also would require formal withdrawal from those agreements.)

States opposed to nuclear weapons probably will not, in the near future at least, undertake the step of withdrawal from the NPT, in part out of cognizance that such an immoderate act may well not suffice to prompt the nuclear powers to undertake negotiations for eliminating nuclear weapons. Another reason is that NPT-withdrawing states would be criticized by a wide spectrum of states, because the "success" of the NPT has kept in world view the prospective attainment of elimination of nuclear weapons. Not only are all but nine states non-nuclear weapon parties to the NPT, but Article VI provides that NPT parties, which include the treaty's five nuclear weapon states, are obliged to "undertake to pursue negotiations in good faith on effective measures relating to cessation of the nuclear arms race at an early date and to nuclear disarmament, and on a treaty on general and complete disarmament under strict and effective international control."

The above conjunction of "nuclear disarmament" and "general and complete disarmament" provides cover for the NPT nuclear weapon states to assert that the NPT supports the view that nuclear disarmament is to be achieved only when and if war-making capabilities are eliminated. Furthermore, today's nuclear weapon states in defense of their weapons-retention policies can cite the NPT Preamble passage, "Declaring their [signatories'] intentions to achieve at the earliest possible date the cessation of the nuclear arms race and to undertake effective measures in the direction of nuclear disarmament." The airy "in the direction of" lends support to the position that the five NPT nuclear weapon states can with legal propriety move at whatever pace they choose in reducing or eliminating nuclear weapons.

States opposed to nuclear weapons are inclined to reiterate that Article VI of the NPT requires pursuit of negotiations on "effective" nuclear disarmament measures "in good faith." The United States in response can call attention to the substantial reductions (mandated at the end of 2012) in deployed strategic warheads of the 2002 Moscow Treaty. Unquestionably, the United States and Russia have reversed their formerly spiraling arms race and have succeeded in eliminating a class of missiles (but not their warheads) with the Reagan-Gorbachev 1987 Intermediate Nuclear Forces Treaty. Nuclear disarmament and good-faith negotiations toward that goal are indeed endorsed and envisioned in the NPT, notwithstanding the treaty's Cold War provenance (1968); but the NPT sets no timetable or deadline for the elimination of nuclear weapons or their reduction.

Other than the above "radical" and ultimately dangerous scenario of withdrawal by non-nuclear weapon states from the NPT (putatively to cause consternation and induce enactment of a worldwide nuclear ban treaty), states might convene an NPT amendment conference, with the goal of amending the treaty so that all its signatories are non-nuclear weapon states. The NPT stipulates of amendments in Article III:

> Any party to the Treaty may propose amendments to this Treaty. The text of any proposed amendments shall be submitted to the Depositary Governments [United States, Britain, Soviet Union], which shall circulate it to all parties to the Treaty. Thereupon, if requested to do so by one-third or more of the parties to the treaty, the Depositary Governments shall convene a conference, to which they shall invite all the parties to the Treaty, to consider such an amendment. (2) Any amendment to this Treaty must be approved by a majority of the votes of all the parties to the Treaty, including votes of all nuclear weapon states party to the Treaty and all other parties which, on the date the amendment is circulated, are members of the Board of Governors of the International Atomic Energy Agency.

For elimination of nuclear weapons, the jutting import above is that all five nuclear weapon parties to the NPT must be among the majority to approve an amendment for purging the treaty of its Article IX(3) provision for "nuclear weapon states"—that is, exploders of a nuclear weapon or device before 1967. If an NPT amendment conference was convened to consider such a step, any of the five NPT nuclear weapon states could scotch the proposed amendment.

States opposed to nuclear weapons know that the requirement of NPT nuclear weapon states' assent to any amendment means an amendment conference almost certainly would not succeed in eliminating the NPT Article IX(3) provision for "nuclear weapon states." An underlying purpose of the conference would be to bring added attention to the problem of the existence of nuclear weapons on Earth. (NPT states hold major review conferences every five years, but no amendment conference has been convened.)

Even supposing that amendment of the NPT was possible without consent of the five NPT nuclear weapon states, simple elimination of the treaty provision for such states would not transform the NPT into an effective vehicle for abolishing nuclear weapons. A ban must be unanimous, but the NPT has not been joined by India and Pakistan and Israel (and North Korea has withdrawn, although it may rejoin). On account of nonunanimity alone, the five most-long-standing nuclear powers would likely hasten to withdraw if the provision for pre-1967 possessors as NPT nuclear weapon states was dropped (or, possibly those states might still just consider and proclaim themselves as nuclear weapon parties, on the principle that an amendment to a treaty must be approved by individual states to apply to them). Today's NPT is also inadequate for eliminating nuclear weapons because it does not mandate prior accession by its parties to the extant chemical and biological weapons bans, which current parties of those agreements, such as the United States, likely will insist upon (see chapter 9). Furthermore, NPT verification (IAEA safeguards on fissionable material of NPT non-nuclear weapon states) does not include challenge inspections initiated by individual states, nor does the NPT require establishment of a national authority (i.e., generally a section or office of a country's State Department or Ministry of Foreign Affairs) to serve as a focal point and liaison under a nuclear ban. Other deficiencies, including the withdrawal provision, contribute to the NPT's broad unsuitability for the worldwide prohibition of nuclear weapons and elimination of current stockpiles. A new treaty is needed to replace the 1968 NPT.

The Vienna Convention on the Law of Treaties in Article 59(1) addresses the demise of a current treaty:

> A treaty shall be considered as terminated if all the parties to it conclude a later treaty relating to the same subject-matter and: (a) it appears from the later treaty or is otherwise established that the parties intended that the matter should be governed by that [later] treaty; or (b) the provisions of the later treaty are so far incompatible with those of the earlier one that the two treaties are not capable of being applied at the same time.

"Incompatible" in (b) is applicable with respect to a nuclear weapons ban treaty replacing today's NPT, if for no other reason than the NPT's nonprohibition of nuclear weapons to a defined set of nuclear weapon states. Section (a) also circumstantiates the NPT's termination, as it will certainly "appear from the later treaty" that it supersedes the NPT. Alternately, nuclear ban drafters could "establish" the termination of the NPT by a statement to that effect in the treaty.

Some states might object, citing extinction of the NPT as leaving them bereft of benefit or possible benefit from the Article IV(2) provision that NPT parties "undertake to facilitate, and have the right to participate in, the fullest possible exchange of equipment, materials, and scientific and technological information for the peaceful uses of nuclear energy." But it is the merits of each case that should determine what assistance and cooperation (if any) states provide to each other, particularly in view of the controversial nature even of peaceful nuclear power. If some states initially see the demise of the NPT as a possible detriment, because of loss of the NPT's cooperation and peaceful assistance injunction, those states most probably will come to realize that this possible loss is more than counterbalanced by the benefits to all people of a world without nuclear weapons. The nuclear powers would be eliminating their nuclear weapons, so other states should be willing to relinquish their NPT claim—and the NPT does not impose specific obligations on individual states—to nuclear assistance from other states. It is sufficient that states let the wheels of humanitarianism, economics, environmental concerns, and energy needs determine the degree of assistance and cooperation on peaceful nuclear energy matters. Today's nuclear powers would certainly favor this position on the issue, and other states should acquiesce, because the NPT's peaceful nuclear cooperation injunction was a trade-off and its main *quid pro quo* (nonprohibition of nuclear weapons to the pre-1967 nuclear powers) would be excluded from a true nuclear weapons ban.

To summarize recommendations so far:

1. The treaty banning nuclear weapons requires signature, ratification, and formal accession by all states before entry into force, which presumptively occurs 180 days after the final state's accession.
2. If a state publicly objects to entry into force within 60 days after the U.N. Secretary-General's announcement that "all states" have joined, entry into force does not occur until the state withdraws its objection and a complete 180-day interval ensues, with no state objecting during the first 60 days.
3. The treaty absolves states of any and all treaty-related obligations before achievement of unanimity and official entry into force—by exempting signatories from Article 18(a) of the Vienna Convention on the Law of Treaties, which adjures states not to defeat a treaty's "object and purpose" after signing but before enough other signatories have accumulated for official entry into force. (The current NPT, under which as signatories the great majority of states have renounced possession of nuclear weapons, remains in force for its parties until the new nuclear treaty takes effect simultaneously for all states.)

4. The treaty is of unlimited duration and declares that the prohibition of nuclear weapons and unsafeguarded fissionable material applies everywhere.

5. The treaty does not permit withdrawal by its parties; but, in accordance with Article 60(2) of the Vienna Convention on the Law of Treaties, a state would not be barred from temporarily disregarding the ban if another state flouted the treaty, in which case under the terms of the nuclear ban the former, "responding" state must publicly designate the initially violating state before undertaking an otherwise treaty-prohibited activity.

6. HEU is blended down over a span of years, with duration depending on Russian-U.S. quantities remaining (including HEU in yet-to-be dismantled weapons) just before commencement of the weapons-elimination period.

7. Challenge inspections initiated by states are an aspect of the verification regime and are carried out (as with today's CWC) unless turned down by three-quarters vote of the nuclear ban's executive council as being frivolous, abusive, or clearly beyond the treaty's scope.

8. The treaty's nuclear weapons-elimination period does not begin until after baseline verification of states' declarations is completed and states vote without demurral that the treaty process should proceed to the next step of weapons elimination (this vote being a judgment on both whether all states have complied with treaty-required declarations and whether all have provided active cooperation to technical secretariat inspectors in their baseline-verification work.)

9. All nuclear weapon states except the United States and Russia must dismantle 25 percent of their warheads within the first three months (90 days) of the elimination period and thereafter need make no further reductions until the United States and Russia, following the timetable's progressively reduced permissible ceilings, reach the other states' respective new, 25 percent lower levels.

To finance the nuclear weapons ban, because all people benefit from a world free of nuclear weapons, all states should contribute to treaty administration and inspection. Mirroring other international agreements, the proposed nuclear ban is financed by assessments based on the ratios of the U.N. dues scale. Assuming the total cost of nuclear ban inspection and administration is as much as $5 billion per year, that is less than 1 percent of the $640 billion fiscal 2008 U.S. defense budget. The U.S. share of a $5 billion nuclear ban budget would be slightly under $1.2 billion, or less than one-quarter of 1 percent of today's annual U.S. defense spending.

The $5 billion is put forward as an "outer limit" figure; the current annual IAEA expense is about $145 million (historically rising, but slowly) for IAEA safeguards applicable to "peaceful-use" fissionable material of NPT non-nuclear weapon states. Predominant additional costs of the worldwide nuclear ban verification regime will be the (1) extension of safeguards (the bolstered safeguards of IAEA INFCIRC/540) to fissionable material, including cores from weapons as they are dismantled, of the five most-longstanding nuclear weapon states and of the non-NPT states (Israel, India, Pakistan, and North Korea); (2) extension of safeguards to plutonium-containing final-disposal sites (insofar as states pursue that) and to uranium-milling (yellowcake) operations;

(3) the international Nuclear Protective Force for guarding plutonium and enriched uranium in transit; and (4) for a time, oversight and accountancy of dismantling of weapons and blending down of HEU to LEU.

Next is the promised discussion of chemical and biological weapons. World-wide prohibition of those instruments will provide a necessary foundation for the elimination of nuclear weapons; and fortunately, substantial progress has already been made.

Prior Prohibition of Chemical and Biological Weapons

The major international barriers to proliferation of chemical and biological weapons include the 1993 CWC (entry into force in 1997) and the 1972 BWC (entry into force in 1975). The United States and Russia are parties to both; also, control regimes such as the "Australia Group" of states aim to restrict the export of chem-bio weapons-usable technologies and material (analogously to the missions of today's Nuclear Suppliers Group and Missile Technology Control Regime). The CWC has the support of the U.S. chemical industry and, in a step beyond inspection by the IAEA for NPT non-nuclear weapon states, CWC verification includes challenge inspections initiated by individual CWC parties—unless contravened by three-quarters vote of the CWC's executive council states.

The 1972 BWC is a much shorter document than the nearly 200-page 1993 CWC, primarily because the BWC lacks verification provisions and does not create a standing regime, as with the overall CWC organization, which is composed of a conference of all parties, an executive council, and a technical secretariat (as would be a nuclear ban treaty). Although BWC terms do not create a standing regime, BWC parties did establish a rudimentary, three-person secretariat in 2007.

The attained ratification of the CWC by the U.S. Senate in 1997 was hard-won, with opponents asking why the United States should pledge to undertake the obligations of the CWC when some other states were not indicating a willingness to do so by joining. With respect to nuclear weapons, if a prospective nuclear ban treaty similarly had an entry-into-force provision of less than unanimity by states, then the greater dangers of nuclear weapons than chemical weapons would propel this argument to *prevail* in certain countries; and lacking unanimity, the nuclear ban would not enter into force.

The CWC required only 65 parties for its entry into force (1997). Now 184 states out of 195 total are CWC parties, and worldwide only five to eight states are generally believed to maintain some level of chemical weapon arsenals (this excluding countries such as the United States and Russia that are still liquidating their arsenals under CWC auspices).

Chemical weapons include phosgene, sulfur mustard, cyanide chloride, and the "nerve agents" sarin and tabun. Agents usable for biological weapons include viruses, representatively Ebola, and bacteria such as tularemia, plague, and anthrax. Among the collective effects of chem-bio weapons are paralysis, coma, death, hemorrhage, blisters, fever, fluid buildup, blindness, and lung damage.

The full name of the BWC is the "Convention on the Prohibition of the Development, Production and Stockpiling of Bacteriological (Biological) and Toxin Weapons and on Their Destruction" (for BWC text, see appendix C). "Toxins," which are produced initially by biological means but are nonliving poisons, include botulinum and ricin. Toxins are also covered by the CWC (see text at www.opcw.org), officially the "Convention on the Prohibition of the Development, Stockpiling and Use of Chemical Weapons and on Their Destruction." The BWC at present has 25 fewer full, ratified signatories than the CWC, but the BWC too has been fully joined by a large (though lesser) majority of the world's states. As with reputed chemical weapons possession, only up to eight states are generally suspected of biological arsenal possession, and those states largely overlap with the suspected chemical weapons possessors.

Chemical weapons pose a smaller-scale threat to human lives than biological weapons, in part because "poison gas" disperses on wind currents, and masks or sealed rooms can bar its effects. For bioweapons, vaccines and antibiotics are the main mitigators of disease and death. Vaccination against one agent does not protect against others, however, and effective treatment of victims of a biological attack requires that the agent be identified quickly enough for prompt treatment of victims, and that the agent not be a permutation of a known virus (in which case current antibiotics would be less effective), and that sufficient antibiotics and medical services be available.

For good reason, anthrax is the most-publicized bioweapon agent. Anthrax in its dry, spore form is hardy, and if microscopically milled (a challenging laboratory task) would be ideal for aerosol dissemination by sprayer on an aircraft. Pulmonary anthrax from airborne exposure can be fatal to humans, whereas anthrax fortunately is not contagious among humans. Other bioweapon-usable agents do cause contagious diseases, but those agents are more likely than anthrax to rapidly degrade and die upon environmental exposure.

In the valuable 1997 U.S. National Academy of Sciences' report "The Future of U.S. Nuclear Weapons Policy," the terminology "weapons of mass destruction" is deemed as somewhat of a misnomer when applied to chemical and biological weapons, at least in comparison to nuclear weapons.[1] The former two classes are abhorrent and in some cases of plausible use could cause widespread human deaths, but the devastatingly effective use of chemical or biological weapons and of truly great loss of life is far less assured than for nuclear weapons. Nuclear weapons also kill by ionizing radiation and firestorm, and destroy life-sustaining hospitals, water supplies, electric power stations, and other infrastructure of cities. Biological and even chemical agents are, however—if successfully weaponized and delivered—wider in their effects on life than conventional armaments on a weight-for-weight basis, so the "mass destruction" appellation probably will endure. (Chem-bio weapons also evoke profound psychological distaste, which tends to perpetuate their categorization along with uniquely baleful nuclear weapons as dread instruments of mass destruction.)

Actual use of chemical weapons in war was renounced by many leading states at the Hague Conference of 1899, where signatories to "Declaration II" promised therein "to abstain from the use of projectiles the sole object of which is the diffusion of asphyxiating or deleterious gases." Chemical weapons as such were at the time largely undeveloped, but the progress of technology presaged their appearance. The states' abjuration of gas warfare was only applicable to the "contracting parties," not states that did not formally subscribe to the declaration. Also, mere possession or stockpiling of asphyxiating or otherwise deleterious "projectiles" was not prohibited, but just their war use.

Another milestone was reached in 1925, with the Protocol for the Prohibition of the Use in War of Asphyxiating, Poisonous and Other Gases, and of Bacteriological Methods of Warfare (the Geneva Protocol). Signatory states to the Protocol agreed "to be bound as between themselves according to the terms of this declaration." Per this, and in line with the 1899 Hague stricture on poison gas, chemical and bacteriological (biological) weapons were not forbidden for use in war against states that had not joined the Protocol and thereby had not renounced their use. Furthermore, and somewhat understandably, about a third of the states assenting to the Protocol did so with a "reservation" rendering the agreement for them only a promise not to be the first to use chem-bio weapons (see chapter 9 for a discussion of "reservations" and the proposed nuclear ban treaty).

The 1925 Geneva Protocol drew its inspiration in part from the use of poison gas in World War I. An indicator of relative "restraint" in that horrendous war can perhaps be seen in each side targeting the other's soldiers, not civilians at large. Also, an argument with effort can be made that gas warfare is less brutal than the use of implements such as machine guns and today's "cluster bombs," because a substantial proportion of gas-attack victims recover from their ordeal and fairly often with less life-altering effects than experienced by survivors of bullets or explosions. Nevertheless, the association of chemical weapons with "poison"—and the potential for these weapons to kill or otherwise victimize innocent noncombatants—has squarely placed chemical weapons among the world's most reviled.

The Protocol's prohibition of war use of chemical weapons was violated by Protocol signatory Iraq during the Iraq-Iran war of the 1980s, and Saddam Hussein's regime also chemically attacked ethnically Kurdish Iraqis in 1987–1988. World response was somewhat muted, for in many Western eyes the Iraqi

Ba'athists were preferable to the Iranian regime after the latter's 1979 theocratic and nationalist revolution (and seizure of Americans as hostages).

Iraq's use of chemical weapons did give fresh impetus to longstanding chemical weapons ban negotiations, and in January 1993 the CWC was opened for states' signatures. Article I of the CWC pledges each state party "never under any circumstances":

> (a) To develop, produce, otherwise acquire, stockpile or retain chemical weapons, or transfer, directly or indirectly, chemical weapons to anyone; (b) To use chemical weapons; (c) To engage in military preparations to use chemical weapons; (d) To assist, encourage or induce, in any way, anyone to engage in any activity prohibited to a State party under this Convention.

Plainly, the CWC far surpasses the 1925 Geneva Protocol's prohibition of use by signatories against one another.

Behind the U.S. Senate's respect-worthy 1997 decision to ratify the CWC, one suspects that there actively lay the knowledge that the United States still has nuclear weapons. Inferential from this is that the United States, and likely the other nuclear powers, in all probability *will not sign a nuclear weapons ban unless all countries agree to non-possession of chemical and biological weapons by joining the extant chemical and biological conventions* (i.e., treaties). Therefore, the proposed nuclear weapons ban treaty by its terms is open for signature only by states that have previously renounced chem-bio weapons by accession to the 1993 CWC and the 1972 BWC.

This requirement could cause some delay in achievement of unanimity for the nuclear ban; but any delay may not be lengthy. Also, consideration is due to what would ensue if CWC/BWC partyship by states was *not* a precondition for signing the nuclear treaty, and therefore one or more countries refused to join (as would be probable). The treaty would have to be withdrawn, be given second life in a version with a provision that only CWC/BWC parties could sign, and be laboriously resubmitted to all states for their evaluation, signature, ratification, and formal accession.

With states having unanimously joined the chemical and biological bans (as a prerequisite for signing the nuclear treaty), any stockpiling of chem-bio weapons would be viewed by the U.N. Security Council as an actionable "threat to the peace." No state can rightfully menace other states by possessing arsenals of weapons *formally renounced by all states*. And as mentioned in chapter 4, the Security Council has U.N. Charter authority to "determine" and act against any "threat to the peace," with or without reference to treaties. The existence of a relevant treaty does, though, increase the likelihood of widely supported Security Council action, and this would be resoundingly so in the case of a unanimously signed agreement.

Today's CWC and BWC both permit withdrawal by parties. The proposed nuclear ban treaty, in addition to requiring states to be parties to the CWC and

BWC before signing the nuclear treaty, includes a provision that nuclear ban signatories *relinquish their right to withdraw from the CWC and BWC once the nuclear ban treaty achieves unanimity of accession by states and officially enters into force.* Such a stipulation of the nuclear ban prevents any state from legally, and therefore relatively easily, withdrawing and proceeding to threaten other states by building or rebuilding an arsenal of chemical or biological weapons. This would be extremely unlikely under the geopolitical force of unanimity, but the possibility of legal withdrawal needs to be cut off by a nuclear ban treaty provision whereby signatories bar themselves from withdrawing from the CWC and BWC. The nuclear treaty proscribes states from (temporarily) disregarding its provisions before making a public declaration of which other state is in material breach of the treaty. A provision of the nuclear treaty *extends this stricture to all states with respect to the CWC and BWC*—so that a state could not clandestinely create or attempt to create chemical or biological arsenals, and *later* claim it did so because such-and-such other state had been in material breach of the CWC or BWC.

Pertaining to the required accession by states to the CWC and BWC before signing the nuclear ban: what if a state joined the CWC, BWC, and nuclear treaty and then, before the latter's achievement of unanimity and entry into force, the state withdrew from the CWC or BWC? This is improbable and would draw criticism, but it would be legal, because states' disavowal of right to CWC or BWC withdrawal does not take effect (as with all nuclear ban provisions) until official entry into force is attained. Consequently, the nuclear ban treaty has a provision that as a condition of entry into force all states must be CWC/BWC parties at the time of the nuclear treaty's entry into force.

The legal capacity of CWC and BWC parties to withdraw from those treaties until the nuclear ban achieves unanimity and enters into force is actually beneficial, because "availability" of withdrawal will facilitate accessions to the CWC and BWC by those states that possess chemical or biological weapons as a supposed, partial counterweight to another state's nuclear arsenal. Today's such-motivated chem-bio possessors might well consent to join the CWC and BWC before signing the nuclear ban only on the condition that they could legally withdraw from the CWC/BWC if, with the passage of significant time, a certain other state or states were retaining their nuclear weapons and showing no signs of movement whatsoever toward joining the nuclear ban treaty. Positing the unlikely, namely that a state joined but then saw fit to withdraw from the CWC or BWC before nuclear ban entry into force, the state could always rejoin the CWC/BWC later and thereby clear the way for nuclear treaty entry into force.

So, when a nuclear ban treaty is introduced for states' signatures, one reason states now possessing chem-bio weapons would have the incentive and a measure of psychic clearance to abjure those weapons (by joining the CWC and BWC) is that the chem-bio renunciation decision *could* be reversed—although *not* at any time after entry into force of the nuclear ban, which as emphasized only occurs after all states have joined the three agreements. Also, the states by renouncing chem-bio weapons would garner praise, with the decision feted as an important step toward global elimination of mass destruction weapons. In addition, renunciation of chem-bio weapons by joining the CWC and BWC would remove an impediment to good relations between the relevant countries and the United States and other important countries. Furthermore, the renouncing countries would have a claim to the moral high ground, in contrast to those that had not (yet) renounced weapons of mass destruction.

Again, only about eight states are generally deemed as probable possessors of chemical or biological arsenals or both. The Arab Republic of Egypt, for example, is believed to hold chemical and possibly biological weapons, and this presumably is in response to Israel's nuclear arsenal (since about 1967). Chemical and even biological weapons do not, however, measure up to nuclear weapons' ineluctability of widespread death, plus infrastructure destruction. If just part of Israel's nuclear arsenal was ever unleashed on Egypt, the loss of life and mayhem wreaked within minutes would be well beyond the ability of relatively feeble chemical weapons (if some survived) to similarly respond. Egypt knows this and therefore subjects Israel's nuclear possession to criticism, but Egypt also holds onto its reputed chemical weapons, because they seem to provide some degree of counterbalance to nuclear weapons. This degree is so relatively slight, however, that the incentives to join the CWC will in all probability become ascendant in Egypt and other of today's reputed chemical possessors—but realistically, this will occur only after the introduction of a nuclear ban treaty for states' signatures. With respect to bioweapons, they in certain imaginable scenarios could destroy numerous lives, too; but the difficulties of wide, effective delivery, and countermeasures that can be taken (vaccine, antibiotics, quarantine), place bioweapons in a different dimension than nuclear weapons.

Israel, in addition to being outside today's NPT, has not acceded to the CWC or BWC; but Israel as with all states would have to fully join the CWC and BWC before joining the new nuclear treaty. (To date, Israel has signed but not ratified only the CWC.) Assuming future, formal renunciation by Israel of chem-bio weapons by accession to the CWC and BWC, Israel *would still have nuclear weapons* until all states have joined the three agreements and the nuclear weapons-elimination period is completed. Egypt, for its part, is a nonnuclear weapon NPT state, as is every country except for the five pre-1967 nuclear powers as well as the nonsignatories India, Pakistan, and Israel, and treaty-dropout North Korea.

The lengthy 1993 CWC contains verification provisions (including challenge inspection), but the short 1972 BWC does not. A nearly seven-year effort by BWC-associated international experts produced a 2001 draft of a BWC "verification protocol," but this was rejected by the United States as too intrusive in some respects and not effective overall.[2]

Although the BWC as is does not include verification, BWC Article VI provides:

(1) Any State party to the Convention which finds that any other State party is acting in breach of obligations deriving from the provisions of the Convention may lodge a complaint with the Security Council of the United Nations. Such a complaint should include all possible evidence confirming its validity, as well as a request for its consideration by the Security Council.

(2) Each State party to this Convention undertakes to cooperate in carrying out any investigation which the Security Council may initiate, in accordance with the provisions of the U.N. Charter, on the basis of the complaint received by the Council. The Security Council shall inform the States parties to the Convention of the results of the investigations.

In evaluating a (posited) future verification protocol instituted for the BWC, some states may with creditable reason choose not to join it—whether due to "intrusiveness," expense, or on a bedrock belief that "worthwhile," creditable biological inspection is impossible; and it is certainly more difficult to achieve or approach than creditable nuclear and even chemical inspection. This distinct possibility of nonunanimous participation in a future biological verification regime (assuming one ever comes to be) underscores the importance of unanimous, formal *renunciation* of biological weapons by all states, with all having joined the BWC as a prerequisite for signing the nuclear ban treaty. Again, unanimity of BWC accession by states would be an unprecedented deterrent to bioweapons development by states, regardless of whether possible future BWC verification is unanimously applied (or whether it even comes to be instituted, which is very much an open question).

During the Cold War, the Soviet Union massively violated the BWC, and it is now told that the Soviets did so upon swallowing the falsity (surprisingly, propagated by certain U.S. operatives) that the United States was flagrantly disregarding the BWC by maintaining a major, covert bioweapons program.[3] For the part of the U.S. military, a sector of it conducts activities using deadly bioweapon agents.[4] Indeed, the BWC in its Article I(1) does not prohibit possession of biological agents except "of types and in quantities that have no justification for prophylactic, protective, or other peaceful purpose"; and such purposes quite possibly can include the development of vaccines and antibiotics (which must be tested against bioweapon-usable agents).[5] Also, a BWC inspection regime if and when instituted presumably could fail to detect a clandestine laboratory, or a pharmaceutical laboratory after an inspection could quickly be converted to production of weapons-usable microbes (the dual-use problem). But even assuming that no future BWC inspection is instituted, the chance of stockpiling or use of bioweapons by states when all have renounced the weapons would be virtually nil because of the geopolitical, psychological, and moral force of unanimity. Currently, with nuclear weapons ready to launch in certain states, it is not surprising that some other, non-nuclear states would pursue chem-bio capability. The United States, a party to the 1993 CWC and 1972 BWC, nobly abjured chemical and biological weapons even before respective introduction for signature of the chem-bio bans, and the United States with similar leadership could choose to express willingness to discuss, on an ongoing international basis, elimination of nuclear weapons under a unanimously joined treaty.

To summarize, the proposed nuclear ban treaty requires states, as a prerequisite for signing the nuclear treaty, to renounce chem-bio weapons by accession to the 1993 CWC and 1972 BWC, and pledges states (once the nuclear ban achieves unanimity and enters into force) not to withdraw from the CWC or BWC (nor from the nuclear ban).

Finally on bioweapons, some opinion holds that the actual danger they pose is greater than that of nuclear weapons, an evaluation giving weight to the easier, more concealable, less expensive production of significant quantities of biological agents (which then for a wide-scale offensive use must be successfully preserved, weaponized, and disseminated). The difficult-to-contain accessibility of biological agents to the likes of terrorists reinforces the importance of all states *renouncing* bioweapons by acceding to the BWC (before signing the nuclear ban), so that the geopolitical force of the prohibition will be extremely strong, and terrorists will have no potential access to weaponized agents from a state's arsenal. Also, states likely would be less prone to harbor terrorists—who might attempt to develop bioweapons—with predictably more intense backlash against those states that do harbor such terrorists, when states without exception have renounced biological (and chemical and nuclear) weapons. It is doubtful, however, that all states will join the CWC and BWC before a nuclear ban treaty is opened for signature, because until that time today's nuclear weapon states have no realistic vehicle to allow them to renounce their nuclear arsenals. With the requirement of accession by states to the CWC and BWC before signing the nuclear treaty, the result upon its entry into force will be worldwide bans on the three classes of weapons of mass destruction.

Chapter 10 examines "reservations," which individual states sometimes include with their accession to a treaty. A reservation is a written pronouncement by a state conveying that one or more provisions of a treaty do not apply to the state as a treaty party, or only under certain conditions or with modification.

Reservations

For two reasons, a treaty banning nuclear weapons cannot allow reservations. First, reservations could weaken the integrity, intended meaning, or application of the worldwide nuclear weapons ban. Second, some states probably would decline to sign the treaty if others, joining later, were at liberty to attach to their accessions various reservations and thereby put earlier-signing states at some disadvantage (whether "real" or simply perceived as such).

Even if reservations are permitted by a treaty, which is the case unless prohibited by treaty terms, Article 19(c) of the Vienna Convention on the Law of Treaties stipulates that any reservation by an acceding state must not be "incompatible" with the treaty's fundamental object and purpose. This, though, is too broadly interpretable for permitting reservations by states when joining a treaty to eliminate nuclear weapons. (Treaties have no adjudicative mechanism whereby an acceding state's reservation, if "incompatible," can be vacated.)

Would the nuclear ban treaty's no-reservations provision be problematic for the United States? Perhaps so, on point of the U.S. Senate's 1997 "Sense of the Senate" declaration that U.S. negotiators to future treaties should not agree to such a provision, nor should the Senate in its treaty ratification role. This issue came to the fore in conjunction with the Senate's ratification of the CWC, which does not permit acceding states to place reservations on its articles, and this was an irritant to some senators. A Sense of the Senate declaration does not, however, carry the force of law or constitutional law, so the U.S. Senate could with legal propriety evaluate and vote on a no-reservations nuclear ban treaty on the basis of the treaty's merits.

It is telling that the Senate in 1997 was not considering so important a matter—elimination of nuclear weapons under unanimous agreement—that its institution by treaty cannot viably allow potentially unequalizing reservations by parties. If a nuclear ban treaty had been a pending reality in 1997, quite possibly the Senate would not have declared as its "sense" that the United States should not henceforth agree in negotiations, nor the Senate in ratification, to a no-reservations provision in treaties. In some cases, it may indeed be a wise course for the Senate to decline to ratify a treaty that forbids reservations, but not for a nuclear weapons ban if it is to be signed by all states.

If official reservations are not permitted, might some treaty parties enact or affirm quasi-reservations on their agreement to join a treaty banning nuclear weapons? And if so, could treaty attainment of unanimity, and thus elimination of nuclear weapons, be put in jeopardy? These questions elicit a close look at the U.S. decision to join the CWC, which prohibits its parties from possessing chemical weapons and was ratified by the U.S. Senate on a 74–26 vote in 1997.[1]

The backdrop of forces leading eventually to Senate CWC ratification included the power of the fact that a state, to participate in important initial measures establishing the CWC regime, needed to join the CWC before it officially entered into force (on April 29, 1997, 180 days after the 65th state's accession, as stipulated in CWC Article XXI for entry into force.) The Clinton administration strongly favored the ban on chemical weapons and was following in the footsteps of the Reagan and successor Bush administrations: in 1990, the United States and the Soviet Union signed their "Agreement on Destruction and Non-Production and on Measures to Facilitate the [prospective] Chemical Weapons Convention." It was a significant step beyond this agreement for the United States to join the multilateral CWC, with its range of required declarations plus verification provisions and financial contributions by parties to support the regime.

The U.S. Senate's resolution ratifying the CWC contained various "conditions," to be construed as structuring the U.S. agreement to join the treaty, and brought to bear on the justification that the U.S. president can "make treaties" only with the "advice and consent" of the Senate. The U.S. Constitution does not specify any Senate prerogative to attach conditions to a treaty ratification resolution, but the Senate with vigor maintains that its constitutional advice and consent can be expressed in this manner. The time pressure in 1997 for U.S. accession before the CWC's entry into force (April 29) enabled CWC opponents and skeptics to wield their influence, which was manifested as various conditions of the Senate's ratification resolution.

The Clinton administration did succeed in parrying away five initially proposed Senate "killer conditions" of the CWC ratification resolution. Because a significant majority of Senators were in favor of the chemical weapons ban, the so-called killer conditions were dispensed by the Senate, resulting in acceptance by the administration of the Senate's ratification resolution (still laden with other conditions, to be summarized shortly).

The first of the five killer conditions struck in due course by the Senate required CWC accession and thus renunciation of chemical weapons, by states such as North Korea, Iran, and the Syrian Arab Republic before the United States joined. The thrust of this condition gives proof again that, for eliminating nuclear weapons, all states will have to join a nuclear ban treaty before its entry into force—or else the United States will say to this effect, "In 1997 we did formally renounce chemical weapons on the multilateral plane by joining the Chemical Weapons Convention; but we absolutely will not renounce nuclear weapons unless all states do likewise."

The second killer condition stipulated that Russia ratify the CWC before its April 29, 1997, date of entry into force, and also required the U.S. president to certify Russian compliance with the aforementioned bilateral 1990 U.S.-Soviet chemical weapons destruction agreement. Russia's elimination of chemical weapons was lagging due to economic problems, and Russia was unable or unwilling to ratify by the date cited, so this was another condition the Clinton administration insisted must be removed (as the Senate eventually agreed; Russia in November 1997 ratified the CWC).[2]

The third condition required the U.S. president to certify that the Central Intelligence Agency could with strong confidence detect "militarily significant" CWC violations. But some quantity of chemical weapons, which are easily created compared with nuclear weapons, conceivably could be surreptitiously produced by a CWC state party, so this condition was also dropped. The Clinton administration argued (and most senators agreed) that the reporting and inspection requirements of the CWC, and the international norm it establishes, would serve as effective barriers to the development of chemical weapons by CWC parties. (Existence of the CWC may also act as a deterrent to non-CWC states that might otherwise develop or retain chemical arsenals.)

The fourth of the five killer conditions originally slated for the Senate's 1997 CWC ratification resolution obliged the U.S. president to bar from U.S. sites CWC inspectors from countries determined by the United States to be sponsors of international terrorism or conveyors of proliferation technologies. This condition eventually was dropped because of the diplomatic difficulties of asserting a blanket privilege to exclude certain inspectors, based solely on their nationality. Article XIII of the CWC, however, does proscribe nationalistic, insidious influence: "In the performance of their duties, the Director-General [of the CWC inspectorate], the inspectors and other members of the staff shall not seek or receive instructions from any Government or from any source external to the Organization" [the CWC-created international "Organization for the Prohibition of Chemical Weapons"].

The fifth killer condition called for changing the CWC by eliminating Article X, "Assistance and Protection Against Chemical Weapons," with it being worrisome to some senators based on the pronouncement that each CWC state party "has the right to request and … to receive assistance and protection against the use or threat of use of chemical weapons." This condition was seen as prejudicial to the principle that any U.S. decision to come to the defense of a country should be made by the U.S. government on a case-by-case basis, and not because action is induced or mandated by U.S. partyship to a treaty (CWC) for banning a certain class of weapons. The CWC does not, however, require its parties to come to the active military defense of a fellow CWC state, with assistance in CWC Article X encompassing "detection equipment and alarm systems; protective equipment; decontamination equipment and decontaminates; medical antidote and treatments; and advice on any of these protective measures." In almost all conceivable cases, the United States would provide medical assistance at least to a country being subjected to chemical attack or threat; but some senators nonetheless objected to Article X's general obligation for CWC parties to aid each other. The United States could not, however, unilaterally alter the negotiated, multilateral CWC, so the condition that Article X be eliminated was also expunged by the Senate from its ratification resolution.

Another section of the fifth killer condition (again, all five "killers" were later removed) called for alteration of CWC Article XI, which states:

> Subject to the provisions of this Convention and without prejudice to the principles of international law, the States parties shall …: (b) Undertake to facilitate, and have the right to participate in, the fullest possible exchange of chemicals, equipment, and scientific and technical information relating to the development and application of chemistry for purposes not prohibited under this Convention; [and] (c) Not maintain … any restrictions … which would restrict or impede trade and development and promotion of scientific and technological knowledge in the field of chemistry for industrial, agricultural, research, medial, pharmaceutical or other peaceful purpose.

The main concern here was that a country might join the CWC, receive cooperation and assistance in developing chemical expertise, and then use it for chemical weapon purposes. But with the CWC being a multilateral treaty in its completed form, it was impossible for the United States to change the above provision, so alteration of Article XI was also dropped from the Senate's ratification resolution (again, because most senators favored joining the CWC).

As noted in chapter 7, the proposed nuclear ban treaty does not have an analogous provision for "peaceful" nuclear energy assistance amongst the world's states. This is not so much for fear that a state would use "peaceful" nuclear expertise or technology for nonpeaceful purpose, because such or any treaty violation would be soundly deterred by the unprecedented geopolitical force of unanimous accession by states to the treaty before its entry into force, and by the benefits to humanity of all states' fealty to the treaty. Notwithstanding, the United States and other countries should not be subject to even a generally worded obligation or expectation to provide nuclear assistance. Supposing there *was* a "peaceful assistance" injunction in the nuclear ban and the United States did not offer such assistance, then in a mild sense the United States would be breaking its word on the treaty, even assuming (as with today's NPT, CWC, and BWC) that specific obligations regarding the amount or nature of peaceful assistance and cooperation are not imposed on parties. (Preeminent "peaceful" use of nuclear energy is electricity from reactors.) The United States and other countries should be able to enter the nuclear treaty with a *clean breast*, not with an implicit undercurrent that "We will provide peaceful assistance in nuclear matters if we wish to, but not if we don't." Countries such as the United States might voluntarily decide to provide peaceful nuclear assistance to others, but its encouragement or obligation would best be omitted from the nuclear ban. (The peaceful assistance provisions of the CWC and BWC would remain, though, in recognition of those two treaties' status as being long established and fully joined by a large majority of states.)

Eventual elimination of the five killer conditions from the U.S. Senate's 1997 ratification of the CWC left those remaining conditions that were ultimately accepted, if not all heartily embraced, by the Clinton administration. The first of the conditions of Senate Resolution 75, "Executive Resolution to Advise and Consent to Ratification of the Chemical Weapons Convention, Subject to Certain Conditions," states the following:

> Upon the deposit of the United States instrument of ratification, the president shall certify to the Congress that the United States has informed all other States-parties to the Convention that the Senate reserves the right, pursuant to the Constitution of the United States, to give its advice and consent to ratification of the Convention subject to reservations, notwithstanding Article XXII of the Convention [which prohibits reservations to the CWC].

Condition 17 below aims to trump no-reservations provisions in future treaties and includes the Sense of the Senate declaration mentioned earlier:

> The Senate makes the following findings: (i) Article II, Section 2, Clause 2 of the United States Constitution states that the President "shall have the Power, by and with the Advice and Consent of the Senate, to make treaties, provided two-thirds of the Senators present concur." (ii) At the turn of the century, Senator Henry Cabot Lodge took the position that the giving of advice and consent to the ratification of treaties constitutes a stage in negotiation on the treaties and that Senate amendments or reservations to a treaty are propositions "offered at a later stage of the negotiation by the other part [Senate] of the American treaty-making power in the only manner in which they could then be offered." (iii) The Executive branch of government has begun a practice of negotiating and submitting to the Senate treaties which include provisions that have the purported effect of (I) inhibiting the Senate from attaching reservations necessary in the national interest; or (II) preventing the Senate from exercising its constitutional duty to give its advice and consent to treaty commitments before ratification of the treaties. (iv) During the 85th Congress, and again during the 102nd Congress, the Committee on Foreign Relations of the Senate made its position clear on this issue when stating that "the President's agreement to such a prohibition cannot constrain the Senate's constitutional right and obligation to give its advice and consent to a treaty subject to any reservation it might determine is required by the national interest."
>
> (B) Sense of the Senate. It is the Sense of the Senate that (i) the advice and consent given by the Senate in the past to ratification of treaties containing provisions which prohibit amendments or reservations should not be construed as a precedent for such provisions in future treaties; (ii) United States negotiators to a treaty should not agree to any provision that has the effect of inhibiting the Senate from attaching reservations or offering amendments to the treaty; and (iii) the Senate should not

consent in the future to any article or other provision of any treaty that would prohibit the Senate from giving its advice and consent to ratification of the treaty subject to amendment or reservation.

Respectfully, however, the kernel of the matter is this: an unalterable insistence by the U.S. Senate that, to be acceptable, treaties must not disallow reservations, and unilateral "amendments" by acceding states would greatly diminish the prospects for abolishing nuclear weapons. If states can attach reservations to their accession to a nuclear ban treaty, then just one state's reservation of any substance would forsake the treaty's necessary, equal applicability to all states. In view of the above-cited 1997 U.S. Senate opposition to no-reservations provisions in treaties, it is ironic that the United States almost certainly would decline to join a nuclear weapons ban treaty if it *permitted* reservations—with their potentially unequalizing force.

In addition to the two conditions concerning reservations, the U.S. Senate maintained in its CWC ratification resolution conditions such as these (summarized): (1) U.S. payments or assistance to the CWC's "Organization for the Prohibition of Chemical Weapons" must be specifically appropriated by Congress; (2) the U.S. president must, before U.S. intelligence information is provided to the CWC Organization, certify establishment of methods to protect intelligence sources; (3) any amendment to the CWC must have the consent of the Senate; (4) the president must certify that the CWC does not undermine U.S. export controls on technology highly usable for chemical weapons; (5) the president must annually report whether U.S. industry is significantly adversely affected by the strictures of the CWC; (6) the president must report at least quarterly to Congressional committees on issues of compliance with the CWC; (7) the president is to ensure that U.S. military forces are protected (to the extent possible) if exposed to chemical weapons; (8) in the event of CWC noncompliance by a CWC state party lasting one year, the president is to consult with the Senate about continued adherence to the CWC (i.e., whether the United States should withdraw); (9) the president must certify that other than medical supplies and treatment, the United States will not provide CWC-related assistance if the parties are sponsors of terrorism; (10) the president must certify that testing of U.S. samples such as soil collected by CWC inspectors will not be conducted outside U.S. territory; (11) the U.S. contribution to the CWC Organization is capped at $25 million per year unless waived by Congress at the request of the president for national security reasons; (12) the president must report to Congress on any additions to the treaty's schedule of chemicals and how such additions may affect U.S. industry and may affect CWC verification; and (13) the president must certify that if an owner of a facility subject to challenge inspection has refused a CWC inspection, a criminal search warrant first must be obtained, and if consent is withheld for routine inspection of a declared facility, an administrative search warrant must be issued before the inspection.

Most of these conditions of the 1997 U.S. Senate ratification resolution are intended to bind the president to keep Congress closely informed on CWC implementation and operation. The final condition could prove distinctly problematic if a search warrant was denied by a U.S. court—notwithstanding that Article VI of the U.S. Constitution cites "treaties" along with the Constitution itself (and laws in its "pursuance") as the "Supreme Law of the Land." Under the CWC, no such case has arisen yet, and it may never will; but the ratification condition of ultimate U.S. court approval for a (disputed) search creates the possibility that a CWC inspection, although in accordance with CWC terms, could not be carried out. (Also problematic is the stipulation that samples only be tested within the United States.)

Positing ratification of a nuclear weapons ban by the U.S. Senate, it is readily conceived that some conditions may be included in its ratification resolution, and that would not be harmful to the treaty if the conditions do not contradict provisions of the treaty. There is, however, another potential trouble spot: domestic (national) implementing legislation. Ill-considered provisions in such legislation, which is required by the CWC and would be by the nuclear ban, could jeopardize the nuclear ban. Unfortunately, Title III ("Inspections") of the U.S. "Chemical Weapons Convention Implementation Act" creates an adverse precedent with the following "national security exception": "Consistent with the objective of eliminating chemical weapons, the President may deny a request to inspect any facility in the United States where the President determines that the inspection may pose a threat to the national security interests of the United States."

A first observation is that one is nonplused as to how denial of a request for inspection under the CWC is "consistent with the objective of elimination of chemical weapons." Second, the words "may pose a threat" open a wide door for denial of inspection. Third, this "national security exception" to CWC inspection contradicts the CWC and is tantamount to a serious reservation (although it escapes that rubric because it is not officially part of the U.S. accession, inasmuch as the CWC does not permit reservations). The CWC declares in Article XIII:

> Each State party has the right to request an on-site challenge inspection of any facility or location in the territory or in any other place under the jurisdiction or control of any other State party for the sole purpose of clarifying and resolving any question concerning possible noncompliance with the provisions of this Convention, and to have this inspection conducted anywhere without delay by an inspection team designated by the Director-General [of the CWC inspectorate] and in accordance with the [CWC] Verification Annex.

Also under CWC Article XIII, any decision to *turn down* a challenge inspection request rests with the CWC executive council, not with an individual CWC state party: "The Executive Council may, no later than 12 hours after having received the inspection request, decide by a three-quarters majority of all its members against carrying out the challenge inspection, if it considers the inspection request to be frivolous, abusive, or clearly beyond the scope of this Convention."

Fourth, a "national security exception" to inspection is not in alignment with the early and logical position of the United States that chemical ban inspection must be strict, or else the ban would be substantially weakened. Also, the U.S. avowal of prerogative to invoke national security exception to inspection may encourage other states to claim the same, although refusal of CWC-authorized inspection is not an option under the terms of the CWC—a treaty voluntarily joined by the United States and other CWC parties. Furthermore, a few countries may not even join the chemical weapons ban, or may sign but delay ratification indefinitely, while claiming that the CWC has been undercut and rendered not worth the trouble.

To be in fundamental compliance with the CWC, the United States will have to repeal the national security exception in the U.S. implementing legislation and also repeal the implementing legislation requirement that samples from U.S. sites must be tested only within the United States. Under the CWC, if on-site testing of a sample yields inconclusive or ambiguous results and requires refined off-site analysis, then a portion of the sample kept under strict chain of custody is to be tested (randomized and double-blinded) at laboratories certified by the technical secretariat of the CWC, which is based not in the United States but at The Hague in the Netherlands.

CWC foibles and sticking points such as these emphasize the importance that—before states' submission of their declarations for a nuclear ban is required—all states' nuclear treaty implementing legislation must be adjudged as acceptable by all fellow treaty parties. (Would today's nuclear weapon states join a prospective nuclear ban if hitherto secret information, such as inventory of nuclear warheads, was mandated to be declared even if states could assert in their implementing legislation a claim to "national security exception" to inspection?)

In addition to deciding on the acceptability of states' implementing legislation for the nuclear ban treaty, its parties—doubtless in consultation with their respective CWC emissaries—would evaluate all fellow states' CWC implementing legislation as to its compliance or noncompliance with the chemical weapons ban. By this standard, the extant U.S. CWC legislation does not pass muster, so at least a few states would deem the U.S. legislation as not acceptable, and by nuclear ban treaty terms its declarations by states would not be required until the United States (and any other then-relevant countries) amended their CWC implementing legislation so that it was CWC compliant, as determined by vote without demurral of all states.

CWC-compliant domestic implementing legislation by all states is not held as crucial on the notion that unalloyed conformity to CWC terms represents the acme of world security (nuclear and even biological weapons are more minatory than chemical), but to facilitate and enhance confidence in a prospective nuclear ban. If a nuclear ban treaty was introduced for signature today, some countries would frowningly say, "The United States, a CWC party since 1997, still maintains its prerogative to refuse CWC inspection. Let the United States first demonstrate basic acquiescence to the CWC, and then we will be able to join the three agreements (CWC, BWC, nuclear ban) prohibiting mass destruction weapons."

Perhaps the United States should not have joined the CWC until the United States was willing to accept the CWC in totality, including its important aspect of inspection. If the United States will join a no-reservations nuclear ban treaty with genuine inspection (which a country cannot refuse), then the United States in all likelihood will see fit to relinquish its currently held prerogative to reject inspection under the CWC, an agreement less critical to people's right to live out their lives.

The discussion rides on the postulates that all states, and notably today's nuclear powers, will sign a nuclear weapons ban only if states first renounce chemical and biological weapons by joining the CWC and BWC (as most have done). But at least a few states probably will refuse to join the prospective nuclear ban if any country maintains an assertion of capacity to invoke a "national security exception" to CWC inspection. The proposed nuclear ban treaty enters into force 180 days after all states have joined (in the absence of objection by a state within the first 60 days and subsequent delay), but the ban's major step of required submission of nuclear declarations is not activated until after all states' domestic implementing legislation for the new nuclear treaty, and for the CWC, is deemed (without demurral) as acceptable, that is, as consonant with and sufficient for those agreements.

To be in conformity with today's CWC, the United States, in addition to eliminating its claim to a "national security exception" to CWC inspection, needs to take the following steps: (1) repealing the provision in the 1998 U.S. CWC implementing legislation that forbids removal of portions of samples from the United States for testing; and (2) rescinding the implementing legislation requirement that U.S. courts must approve a (disputed) inspection request—as of a chemical plant—even though duly authorized by the CWC regime (this U.S. statutory stipulation derives from one of the Senate's conditions for ratification). The granting of ultimate decision on this matter to the U.S. courts amounts to a reservation of substantial impact and would, if claimed for a nuclear ban treaty, prevent accession by states.

It could be surmised that U.S. departure from the CWC's terms in some aspects of CWC implementing legislation can be traced to the general unease associated with opening one's sovereign country to inspection, even absent any present or planning wrongdoing. In addition, the CWC is not unanimously joined, so the moderate level of discomfort linked to "inspection" is aggravated by ongoing awareness that several states have not formally renounced chemical weapons by joining the chemical weapons ban. Under the proposed nuclear ban, before its entry into force the CWC (and BWC) must attain unanimous accession by states; but if any state(s) attempted to hamstring the nuclear ban treaty by untoward provisions in domestic implementing legislation, or contradicted the CWC through such legislation, then the nuclear ban's requirement of declarations would not take effect until the legislation was changed by the state(s) and met acceptance by all fellow states. With all states posited as having joined the nuclear treaty and prior to that the CWC (and BWC), the prospect of relentless international censure would militate against any state delaying or preventing implementation of the nuclear treaty by enactment or stubborn maintenance of contradictory implementing legislation for the nuclear ban or the CWC.

The sharp focus on the United States in this chapter calls for balanced awareness that the United States was a crucial contributor in drafting the arduously conceived CWC. Also, the U.S.-Soviet renunciation of chemical weapons was put to paper in 1990, even before the CWC was opened for signature (1993), and the U.S. Senate in 1997 ratified the CWC although it required only 65 states as parties for entry into force. Furthermore, there is no reason to believe that the United States will ever flout its word as a CWC party by rebuilding a stock of chemical weapons, and the United States to date has not refused a CWC inspection and may well never do so (and, interestingly, so far no CWC state has seen need to avail itself of a challenge inspection).

If the United States continues for a time to maintain its asserted "national security exception" to inspection under CWC auspices, that would not be fatal to the goal of banning nuclear weapons. It is possible that only the introduction of a feasible nuclear ban treaty will induce a country to change a contradictory provision in extant CWC implementing legislation, which is to say the *incentive* of attainable freedom from the nuclear weapons threat might be necessary.

Conceivably, a state could later amend its domestic legislation to contradict the enacted nuclear ban (or the CWC). Such an act would be akin to a breakout and would be deterred, if ever contemplated, by the certainty of worldwide opposition and outrage—because all states joined the treaty, the treaty is in force, and it benefits all people.

To summarize, just before entry into force (1997) of the CWC, with its no-reservations provision, the U.S. Senate adopted a posture of strong disapproval of future no-reservations treaties. This was appropriately manifested as a Sense of the Senate declaration, which by its nature would not legally interdict the executive branch nor the Senate from consideration of a no-reservations nuclear ban treaty. The proposed nuclear ban treaty, in addition to stipulating (before states' submission of nuclear declaration) that all states accept fellow states' treaty implementing legislation, requires such acceptance of states' CWC implementing legislation.

Elimination of nuclear weapons necessarily will require inspections that are applicable in full to all parties, or the United States for one would decline to sign the treaty, with any country able to reject inspection or some aspect of it. On the premise that the United States will join a nuclear ban treaty and do so with the intention of complying with its inspection and other provisions, then the United States (and other relevant countries) likely would see fit to bring their CWC implementing legislation into compliance with the CWC (before which time dismantling of nuclear warheads would not begin).

Countering Near-Earth Objects

A potential stumbling-block to worldwide elimination of nuclear weapons attaches to the specter of a Near-Earth Object (NEO) approaching our planet, and the conceivable use of nuclear-tipped missiles to obliterate the object or divert its course. Myriad asteroids nonthreateningly orbit the Sun along the Asteroid Belt between Mars and Jupiter; but an asteroid could be altered in its course and possibly pose a threat to Earth by a collision among asteroids, or, over time, by the Yarkovsky Effect (the small push on an object when some of its absorbed solar radiation flies back into space).

In 1908 in Siberia an object exploded and vaporized in the air (no crater was made), flattening miles of forest. About 50,000 years ago a 100- to 150-foot object slammed into northern Arizona, creating the 4,000-foot diameter Barringer ("Meteor") Crater. Other crater outlines held to be of cosmic (not volcanic) origin have been discovered, and it is axiomatic among researchers that evidence of additional impacts has been erased by erosion and weather.

A second set of potentially unwelcome visitants are comets (from the Greek, "hairy star"), gas-emitting masses containing carbon, hydrogen, oxygen, and nitrogen, the presence of which essential elements of life has given rise to theories that comets originally brought organic matter to Earth. Comets are thought to have been born 4–5 million years ago, when our solar system began to coalesce.

If a comet hit the earth's atmosphere, the comet's 40,000-plus miles-per-hour velocity could generate sufficient heat to cause immolation. It is sobering to consider, however, that a giant comet might break through relatively unscathed. Fortunately, the vast majority of cosmic objects are small enough to burn up by friction or harmlessly explode if they do hit the earth's protective blanket.

An asteroid is generally deemed to be "large" if it is at least one-half mile wide. A 500-mile-wide asteroid ("Ceres") was the first discovered, in 1801, but most asteroids are much smaller and many are just the bulk of a car or a bus. A large asteroid smashing into Earth would have extremely damaging results, including submersion of vast coastal areas if an ocean was struck.

A collision of cosmic objects was vividly demonstrated in 1994 with the barrage of breaking-up Comet Levy-Shoemaker 9 into Jupiter, our planetary system's giant and a gravity-bearer of such mass that it functions somewhat as a "suction device" to approaching objects (protecting Earth to a degree). To strike back at an Earth-approaching asteroid or comet, nuclear warhead-loaded missiles are envisioned as destroying the object, or deflecting its course through detonations off the bow.

U.S. scientists announced in September 2000 that the NEAR (Near-Earth Asteroid Rendezvous) spacecraft then orbiting the 26-mile-wide, potato-shaped asteroid Eros transmitted data proving that Eros is of hard-rock composition, although with some interior cracks—perhaps from collisions with fellow asteroids. All asteroids may not be of like firmness, but exploding a unitary mass such as Eros would be more difficult than accomplishing the same thing with a rubble pile. The superb scientific and engineering achievement of NEAR (and the seven-year "Stardust" mission to and from comet Wild 2) is not indicative that interception, much less successful destruction or diversion, of a newly discovered NEO in relative proximity to our planet would be easy; the farther away an NEO is the more time is available to track its trajectory with increasing precision.

It would be unwise to propose that an internationally controlled stock of warheads (or, as they would be termed, "nuclear explosive devices") be retained under the nuclear ban for an attempted liquidation of a threatening NEO. The lead time of a year, and preferably much longer for a credible attempt, and the much shorter time required to create nuclear warheads, militates against the necessity of keeping prefabricated, nearly completed "devices" or warheads. (In the United States, the National Aeronautics and Space Administration is leading an effort to find and track asteroids.)

Even if there was international guardianship and ownership of some nuclear "devices," they would need to be refurbished over time, which many generate security concerns. Also, some states might be wary that a large state could launch an assault on the international nuclear repository and suddenly be in possession of "devices" separate from warheads in name but not function. The apprehension of this scenario may be ineradicable, although any such an execrable breakout from the nuclear ban would be (speaking of the skies) astronomically unlikely, with this again attributable to the geopolitical force of unanimous accession by states to the treaty, as well as the benefits to all states of a nuclear weapons–free world.

An internationally controlled nuclear warhead stockpile should not be maintained for possible Earth-bound purposes, that is, as military weapons. Security questions would always exist, and if the weapons' use was ever contemplated, the decision ultimately would turn on a majority vote of member states of the U.N. Security Council. This would mean, however, that against the wishes of other (outvoted) countries, nuclear weapons might be put into action. Also, with the great majority of states not being among the five permanent Security

Council members with veto power, the former mass of states probably would reject a regime wherein potential use of nuclear weapons was codified in the nuclear ban. The prime reason for eliminating nuclear weapons is to liberate humanity from the threat of their lethal harm, and this aspiration would be shaken in perpetuity by any ongoing, even internationalized retention of the instruments for potential war use.

An attempt to deal with a threatening NEO, however, does not constitute "war use." Under the proposed nuclear ban treaty, could nuclear explosion technology be used in an effort to avoid an NEO catastrophe? Yes, with a treaty provision allowing temporary creation of "nuclear explosive devices," with special authorization by the treaty's executive council.

World leaders would consult with rare avidity in the event of a NEO crisis. Probably, the United States and a few other individual countries, or an ad hoc consortium of countries, would request authorization from the nuclear ban's executive council to create some nuclear explosive devices.

In this contingency of a large object bearing down and threatening Earth's inhabitants, the nuclear ban's executive council would authorize—for short duration and with full transparency—any reasonable request of this nature.[1] "Reasonable" here presupposes considerable international scientific testimony that the NEO is of dangerous size and that its trajectory poses a distinct threat to Earth.

In brief, the nuclear ban treaty permits time-limited production of nuclear explosive devices to counter a specific NEO threat, with authorization and direct oversight by the treaty's executive council. The treaty, however, does not permit use of nuclear explosion technology for other purposes (excavation, oil exploration). The appeal of such projects had waned by 1991, as then noted by the United Nations: "The original optimism on the possible benefits of PNE [peaceful nuclear explosion] technology has now been reversed. The combination of environmental problems, delicate arms control issues, cost and security and safety problems have all contributed to a common understanding that PNE technology is generally impractical."[2] In the past, Russia and China particularly espoused the potential benefits of PNE, but now those countries have muted such claims.

This and other contemporary discussion of NEOs and nuclear explosive devices may prove moot, insofar as nuclear explosions are not the only possible countermeasures to an NEO threat. Nascent or unborn technologies such as giant laser beans, solar sails, and "gravity tractor" spacecraft may in the future be seen as more promising than attempting to intercept and explode an NEO—which, if imperfectly accomplished, could create even greater destruction on Earth through multiple hits by still-large fragments. In any case, a given 100-year span poses only an estimated 1 in 5,000 chance of a strike by a catastrophic, kilometer-wide or greater asteroid.[3] A comet strike is even less statistically threatening, due to relative scarcity of comets in our cosmic neighborhood.

"Societal verification," the next subject, has long and honorably been advanced as a means to further ensure states' compliance with a treaty by additionally deterring, through even greater risk of exposure, any attempt at surreptitious treaty violation. Societal verification would be an adjunct to the nuclear ban treaty regime (see chapter 5) of systematic (routine) and special inspections, and challenge inspections initiated by individual states.

Societal Verification

Perhaps the most obvious measure to support societal verification is a fund for rewarding a provider of valid information about nuclear ban treaty noncompliance. Such a fund, however, would best not be maintained under treaty endorsement or administration, in deference to the worldwide ban's pure and nonpecuniary purpose of freeing humanity from the threat of nuclear war and diminishing to asymptotically near-zero the risk of nuclear terrorism (the latter achieved by eliminating current warheads, which could be stolen or diverted, and blending down HEU to LEU). But, existence of a reward fund could conceivably provide motivation for someone to report a here-posited (though most unlikely under a unanimous treaty) treaty violation, so the role of a fund should not be ignored. A reward fund also would serve as an aid to some states in joining the ban, with higher confidence engendered that any attempt at cheating by a state would be reported and exposed. At the time when a nuclear ban treaty is introduced for states' signatures, an entity such as a U.S. philanthropic foundation could disseminate to media and post on the Web a message similar to this:

> The [name] Foundation has long supported work for international peace and goodwill. At present, the world stands at the dawn of a process which, once all states have joined the nuclear ban treaty, is set to culminate in elimination of nuclear weapons.
>
> We believe that attempted cheating on a unanimous treaty is extremely unlikely. Notwithstanding, to further solidify the assuredness of fealty to the treaty, the Foundation has established a fund for the purpose of rewarding "whistle-blowers" who may reveal treaty violation. The fund will stand at approximately $10 million, and its earning will be remitted annually to UNICEF.
>
> Disbursement of any or all of this reward fund will be solely at the discretion of the Foundation. We expect no treaty cheating, but if it occurs, we are ready to disburse major reward for its revelation.

Although the nuclear treaty regime would not function to authorize or administer rewards to whistle-blowers, the treaty's executive council would make the ultimate decision as to whether a received "report" had the credibility to warrant a special inspection. (The nuclear ban's executive council has seats for perhaps 30–35 rotating states from the world's geographic areas, as well as permanent seats for the pretreaty nuclear powers.[1])

Almost certainly, the U.S. government and some others would announce their own rewards for whistle-blowing. The more proclaimed sources of deserved largess the better—to increase the extent to which persons in a position to reveal a treaty violation would be confident that reward from one or more sources for significant, valid information about treaty noncompliance would be forthcoming. The U.S. government might offer on the order of $100 million; after all, a reasonable expectation under a unanimous treaty is that no treaty violation would occur—and if a violation did occur, a payout of millions of dollars would be a pittance compared with the importance of disclosure of treaty violation. Although some persons may be impervious to even stratospheric financial inducement, others would not, and this "uncertainty factor" would act as a barrier to any move by a state pursuant to a (here-supposed) inclination to attempt to secretly violate the unanimously joined treaty.

Next, and as is often proposed for "societal verification," the nuclear ban treaty should adjure in general terms states to provide asylum for persons and their families who may be endangered by revelation of nuclear ban cheating. As with the existence of reward funds, the prospect of asylum offered by states can only increase the willingness of citizens worldwide to engage in whistle-blowing of a treaty violation. (Whistle-blowing could be initially anonymous, with a reference number established by the receiving party—the executive council or technical secretariat of the overall treaty organization, or the state or foundation offering a reward.)

Moving to a third element to enhance societal verification, the nuclear ban treaty should mandate enactment of penal legislation as part of states' treaty-required domestic implementing legislation and incurring criminal penalties for activities (such as by individuals or a terrorist gang) prohibited under the ban. Article VII of the CWC already requires such:

> Each State party shall, in accordance with its constitutional processes, adopt the necessary measures to implement its obligations under this Convention. In particular, it shall: (a) Prohibit natural and legal persons anywhere on its territory … from undertaking any activity prohibited to a State party under this Convention, including enacting penal legislation with respect to such activity.

U.N. Security Council Resolution 1540, adopted April 2004, has a similar adjuration to states, but it should be specified in and for the nuclear ban treaty.

Regarding *state* activity, should the nuclear ban pronounce it to be the "right and duty" of citizens to report (to the treaty regime) prohibited nuclear activity? This may seem useful in bolstering societal verification, but such a provision would also widen the psychological window for conveyance of false reports by crackpots, factions, or others in a state. If called to task or apprehended for allegedly making a false and malicious report, the perpetrator could claim, "Wait a minute. I acted in good faith. You can't prove I didn't. The nuclear ban says our right and duty is to report suspected violations. Let me out of here!" Considering then a much different case, in which a genuinely righteous individual was willing to undergo risk by reporting on actual treaty-prohibited activity by his or her state, a nuclear ban pronouncement of a "right and duty" to report would likely do nothing to enhance the safety of the discloser of a violation given the nature of the state's governing regime that might (to imagination anyway) flout a treaty joined by all states.

Next, the nuclear ban treaty advisedly should not proclaim that nuclear weapons development or possession by a state is a "crime" or a "crime against humanity." This recommendation hinges on the fact that it cannot be absolutely and antecedently proven that no state would ever violate the treaty; and response to a definitive nuclear ban "breakout" is a circumstance under which (temporary) development of nuclear weapons should not be considered or intoned as a "crime." Moreover, a crime or criminal designation in the treaty of nuclear possession by a state quite possibly would be taken by today's nuclear weapon states as casting unacceptable and unnecessary aspersion on their "historical" (pretreaty) status as possessors of war-ready nuclear arsenals.

The acknowledgment that permanent adherence to the ban by all states cannot be absolutely proven is not per se problematic. It also cannot be absolutely proven, for example, that three-fourths of the world population will not, on a certain date, simultaneously stand on one foot for three minutes. One can *conceive* of a state overtly breaking out of a unanimous ban (or attempting to surreptitiously violate it), just as one can conceive of three-fourths of all people together standing on one foot for three minutes. With a nuclear weapons ban that is joined by all states before entry into force and that is fair to all states, the chance of a material breach is miniscule at most and would be met, if it occurred, by concerted opposition from all spheres of the international community.

To summarize on measures related to "societal verification":

1. The nuclear ban treaty does not label it a "crime" or a "crime against humanity" for a state to develop or possess nuclear weapons, this in deference to the sensibilities of today's nuclear powers, and in light of the *presumed* possibility that a state might at some time break out of the treaty—in which case temporary, reactive nuclear development by another state(s) could not rightfully be branded a crime (but recall the nuclear ban requirement that a state must name whatever other state is in material breach before undertaking an otherwise treaty-prohibited activity, and to avoid world castigation and possible other consequences would need to present sufficient evidence to credit the charge).

2. Regarding treaty-prohibited, nuclear weapons–related activity (as by an individual or terrorists), the treaty requires states to enact penal provisions as part of domestic implementing legislation.

3. The treaty does *not* establish a fund for rewarding whistle-blowers; but it is likely that the United States and other countries would do so, and possibly also entities such as foundations.

4. To avoid providing protective incentive for hoax or other baseless reports, the treaty does *not* declare it to be the "right and duty" for citizens to report a state's (here-posited) treaty-prohibited activity.

5. The treaty in general terms calls upon its parties to offer asylum to anyone and their families who may be in jeopardy because of the revelation of a treaty violation.

Elimination of nuclear weapons will be at least as beneficial to today's nuclear powers as to others, yet the former will approach a prospective treaty with more wariness than states in general. Therefore, societal verification provisions that might cause serious discomfiture for the nuclear powers should be avoided in the treaty, to facilitate its achievement of unanimous accession by states.

While affirming the above, it is still realistic to envision that under the nuclear ban "societal verification" will be *profoundly operative*—even though the treaty does not proclaim possession of nuclear weapons by states to be a "crime," nor declare citizens' reporting to be a "right and duty." Persons everywhere will know that the unanimously joined nuclear weapons ban is in effect, and the chance of the posited treaty violation being reported by a citizen or worker-citizen is great—because there are men and women of conscience worldwide, and elimination of nuclear weapons benefits all humanity. In addition, the prospect that a defector or other revealer of treaty violation would be lauded internationally and be eligible for outstanding financial reward would enhance the workings of societal verification and additionally deter any undertaking by a state to surreptitiously violate the treaty. Today, though, conditions are much less conducive to whistle-blowing of a covert nuclear program, and this is fundamentally because the weapons are not outlawed worldwide, certain states avowedly possess them, and possession is not prohibited to the four non-NPT states nor to the five NPT states that became possessors of nuclear weapons before 1967.

Other Matters

At this juncture it may useful to review the major steps that must be accomplished *before actual commencement of warhead elimination*, under the proposed treaty (some of these overlap; the first step has already been met by a large majority of states):

(1) States not already parties to the 1993 CWC and the 1972 BWC join those treaties (as a prerequisite for signing the nuclear ban), and thereby pledge not to develop or possess chemical and biological weapons.

(2) 180 days after "all states" have joined the nuclear ban treaty, as announced by the U.N. Secretary-General, the treaty enters into force—unless a state calls for delay within the first 60 days, in which case the incipient interval is annulled and a new such interval toward entry into force commences whenever the state withdraws the objection.

(3) (a) Once the treaty enters into force, all states enact domestic (national) implementing legislation for the treaty covering such matter as access for inspectors and designation of the states' nuclear ban National Authority.

    (b) All states enact CWC implementing legislation.

    (c) The states' implementing legislation enactments are submitted to fellow treaty parties for their evaluation as to adequacy and compatibility with their respective treaties.

    (d) States vote, without demurral, that the enactments are "acceptable."

(4) States submit to the nuclear ban technical secretariat their treaty-required declarations of nuclear material, facilities, and weapons.

(5) The technical secretariat undertakes, completes, and reports to states on its baseline verification of declarations.

(6) States vote (without demurral) that the treaty process should "proceed to the next step" of weapons elimination.

(7) 30 days later the treaty's timetable of phased reductions of nuclear warheads begins.

According to number 3, a single state could "hold up" (without limitation of time) the treaty's "declarations" requirement, and under number 6, any state could hold up commencement of weapons elimination (the heart of the treaty). But with all states having acceded to the nuclear ban treaty, its geopolitical momentum in all likelihood would dissuade any state from insouciantly giving reason for another state to cast a vote that would delay the steps of submission of declarations and the start of weapons elimination.

At present, multilateral negotiations for a treaty banning nuclear weapons have not commenced. The Geneva-based international Conference on Disarmament (C.D.) operates by consensus among its currently 65 member countries, so the C.D.'s potential and appropriate use as a nuclear abolition forum can be blocked by a few countries or even just one. If nuclear weapons ban activity by the C.D. does not prove forthcoming, the following two approaches are possible:

> The world community could decide to take matters into its own hands, as it did in the "Ottawa Process" as regards anti-personnel land mines. Any state or group of states could invite other states to a conference to agree on a treaty or course of action.... [or] Since the U.N. General Assembly unanimously decided that the United Nations "has a central role and primary responsibility in the sphere of disarmament," the General Assembly has the authority and power to create whatever forums it deems necessary.... It can, if it so decides, also make any recommendations or requests by a simple or two-thirds majority vote, to any state or group of states or forum.[1]

Suppose that an assemblage of countries utilized a U.N. group or similar forum to give birth to a prospective nuclear weapons ban. (Any such effort would draw heavily on the extant Model Nuclear Weapons Convention; see analysis of that document in appendix A.) The United States possibly would ignore the effort or pronounce it futile; but with the passage of time, the U.S. attitude might change, and from the start all countries' policymakers (including those in the United States) would study the proceedings and substance of progress. Also, the United States or other nations might decide to join negotiations at any time.

Perhaps, though, one or more "important" countries would stand aloof throughout the process, and the treaty would be finalized and introduced for signatures without their substantial or official input. This would not ruin the treaty's prospects if the treaty makes it as easy as possible for the nuclear weapon states to join, by requirements such as unanimous accession before entry into force, prior accession by states to the chem-bio bans (CWC/BWC), nonwithdrawal from the nuclear ban (plus CWC and BWC), necessity of vote without demurral by states of acceptability of fellow states' domestic implementing legislation before nuclear declarations must be submitted to the treaty regime, and requirement (after baseline verification of declarations) that states vote without demurral that the treaty process should proceed to the next step. Thus, even if some countries stood apart from the negotiations (or their beginning stage), that does not mean those countries would not join a finalized treaty, as addressed by Daisaku Ikeda:

> Only some of the nuclear weapons powers were involved in formulating the Non-Proliferation Treaty [NPT], but consistent effort eventually resulted in participation of all five longstanding nuclear powers, plus states thought to be nuclear-capable … As this process suggests, taking the initiative in working on a treaty can encourage nuclear weapons powers and their allies to free themselves from their nuclear dependence.[2]

(NPT "participation" by the NPT nuclear weapon states preeminently includes Articles I and III pledges not to provide nuclear weapons or unsafeguarded fissionable material to other states.) Canadian statesman Douglas Roche has written that the nuclear weapon states "must be encouraged to accept the growing global wisdom that the security of all States would be improved in a nuclear weapons–free world."[3]

The following highlights testify that U.S. presidents have not been oblivious to the dangers of weapons of mass destruction. President Eisenhower in 1953 proposed the Atoms for Peace program, thereby stimulating creation (1957) of the IAEA that today safeguards peaceful-use fissionable material of NPT non-nuclear weapon states. (The philosophy of Atoms for Peace is not immune to criticism, insofar as encouragement of peaceful nuclear technology dissemination may increase the risk that technology will be used to develop nuclear weapons— at least in the absence, as today, of a worldwide nuclear weapons ban.) President Kennedy signed the 1963 Partial Test Ban Treaty, and implemented with the Soviet Union the "hot line" communications link, and spoke tellingly to the world of the nuclear "sword of Damocles." President Johnson's administration completed negotiation of the NPT; under President Nixon, the NPT and the U.S.-Soviet Strategic Arms Limitation Talks (SALT I) "interim accords" (limiting launchers and antiballistic missile systems) were signed. Also, the United States renounced biological weapons in 1969, before the introduction of the BWC for signature in 1972. President Carter signed SALT II, and after office (1998) he joined 116 other world civilian leaders who issued a call for de-alerted nuclear weapons, worldwide halt to the production of new fissile material for weapons, permanent cessation of nuclear test explosions, deep reductions in U.S.-Russian arsenals (to be achieved to a significant degree by the end of 2012 under the 2002 Moscow Treaty), commitment by the other nuclear states to reduce their arsenals, and pursuit of the "final goal of elimination."[4]

President Reagan's great dream was elimination of nuclear weapons,[5] and he and Soviet President Gorbachev achieved this for a class of missiles—but not their warheads—with the 1987 Intermediate-range Nuclear Forces Treaty.[6] (Gorbachev spoke in favor of abolition of nuclear weapons at the United Nations on January 15, 1986.) President G. H. W. Bush in 1991 signed START, which limited "accountable" deployed strategic U.S. and Soviet warheads to 6,000 per side by December 5, 2001, and he cut off U.S. production of fissile material for weapons, de-alerted some ICBMs, and instituted major withdrawals from deployment and de-activation of most U.S. nonstrategic nuclear weapons. During President Clinton's tenure, the United States acceded to the CWC, U.S. funding of Congressionally-initiated Cooperative Threat Reduction and allied programs increased, and the Comprehensive Test Ban Treaty was signed (but not ratified). President G. W. Bush, along with Russian President Vladimir Putin, in May 2002 signed the Strategic Offensive Reductions Treaty (the Moscow Treaty), which mandates reduction at the end of 2012 of each countries' deployed strategic warheads to a maximum of 2,200, almost two-thirds below the 6,000 START limit.

Some may claim that elimination of nuclear weapons is not really important or necessary, because the world in all probability will see no nuclear showdown or future use of nuclear weapons. This assertion can be deemed credible only if present and future "states of concern" never, over the course of time, develop (and use) nuclear weapons, and false-alarm missile launch never occurs, and no "minor" or border war escalates into nuclear use, and a preemptive strike against nuclear weapons or facilities does not result in nuclear counterattack, and "loose nukes" or HEU do not find their way into the hands of terrorists. Should humanity cast its lot with these uncertainties, or bring to reality a treaty that embodies the unprecedented geopolitical, psychological, and moral force of unanimous accession and liberates present and future generations from the nuclear weapons threat?

As written by the Buddhist sage Nichiren (b. Japan 1222 c.e.), in his missive *The Gift of Rice*, "Life itself is the foremost of all treasures.... Even the treasures that fill the major world system [i.e., "galaxy"] are no substitute for life."[7] And if, as taught in the Bible (and other scriptures), a merciful Supreme Being created the universe and life, then how can the vast and indiscriminate power of death inherent in weapons of mass destruction be seen as other than contrary to scriptural basis?

Summary

The following is a summary of recommendations for an effective treaty to ban nuclear weapons:

1. The proposed nuclear weapons ban treaty enters into force 180 days after all states have signed and ratified it and deposited their instruments of accession with the depositary (the U.N. Secretary-General). "Unanimous accession by states" is presumptively established when the Secretary-General announces that "all states" have joined; but within 60 days thereafter, any state can rescind the 180-day interval leading to entry into force—if, for example, an ambiguous or "ungoverned" area presents a perceived nuclear threat. Whenever any objection is withdrawn, a new 180-day interval toward entry into force commences (and again with a 60-day window for objection).

2. The treaty provides that, notwithstanding Article 18(a) of the Vienna Convention on the Law of Treaties, nuclear ban signatories have no obligations whatsoever under the treaty until all states join and it officially enters into force. The current NPT, under which as signatories the vast majority of states have renounced nuclear weapons and possession of unsafeguarded fissionable material, remains in effect during accumulation of nuclear ban accessions.

3. (a) Only states already parties to the extant conventions prohibiting chemical and biological weapons (CWC/BWC) can sign the nuclear ban (so that elimination of nuclear weapons is preceded by worldwide extension of the chem-bio bans).

   (b) Entry into force of the nuclear ban treaty does not occur unless all states are at the time CWC/BWC parties (this to address the possibility that a state could join the CWC/BWC and then join the nuclear ban but drop out of the CWC or BWC before the nuclear ban's achievement of unanimous accession and entry into force; but in that case, the "dropout" could rejoin the CWC/BWC and thereby clear the way for nuclear ban entry into force, with all states being parties to the three treaties).

4. Reservations by states to the treaty are not permitted (because they could weaken the intended meaning or application of the worldwide treaty, and because some states might decline to sign the treaty out of apprehension that later signatories would attach unequalizing reservations to their individual accessions).

5. The warhead elimination period does not begin until (a) states enact their domestic implementing legislation for the treaty, plus such legislation for the CWC; (b) states accept without demurral their fellow states implementing legislation; (c) states submit declarations of nuclear material, facilities, and weapons; (d) the nuclear ban technical secretariat completes and reports on its baseline verification of declarations; and (e) states vote without demurral that the treaty process should proceed to the next step.

6. The duration of the nuclear weapons [warhead] elimination period (3, 4, or 5 years) is contingent on the greater quantity of U.S. or Russian warheads at the time, following verification of declarations, that states vote without demurral that the treaty's next step of weapons elimination be taken.

7. If during the elimination period one-quarter of the executive council states vote that a state is not in compliance, the time-bound progress of the elimination period is suspended until by consensus council vote the noncompliance is found to have been rectified.

8. All states possessing nuclear warheads, with the exception of Russia and the United States, must eliminate 25 percent of their warheads within the first three months of the weapons-elimination period. Thereafter, during the time-bound progression toward zero, states may discontinue dismantling warheads until Russia and the United States have reached the varying, much lower levels of the other nuclear weapon states.

9. Withdrawal from the enacted nuclear weapons ban is not permitted.

10. The treaty pledges states not to withdraw from the CWC and BWC, so that all states are permanently parties to the three agreements banning weapons of mass destruction.

11. If, in response to a material breach by a state, another state or states under the aegis of Article 60(2) of the Vienna Convention on the Law of Treaties undertakes otherwise-prohibited activity, the "responding" state must declare beforehand which state it arraigns as in material breach and must also declare when the breach is held to no longer exist, after which time the responding state must fully recomply with the treaty. (A material breach of, for example, the CWC would never allow a state to ignore the nuclear ban or BWC; the agreements are separate legal documents, and otherwise-prohibited activity could be temporarily undertaken only in regards to the corresponding one of these treaties that was being violated by another state.)

12. (a) The nuclear ban treaty provides that states will offer asylum to a person or persons and their families who are in possible jeopardy for revealing treaty violation.

    (b) As part of domestic implementing legislation, states must enact penal provisions for treaty-prohibited acts. (The treaty does not, however, establish reward funds for "whistle-blowers," although the odds are great that various states will do so.)

13. (a) The treaty verification regime includes challenge inspections that can-
       not be lawfully refused by state fiat or national court.

    (b) Full access by inspectors to suspect sites is required; but as with
        today's CWC, an individual state's challenge inspection of another
        state's site is subject to denial by three-quarters executive council vote
        if determined by such margin to be frivolous, abusive, or clearly
        beyond the treaty's scope.

    (c) The treaty provides for declaration by inspectors of temporary exclu-
        sion zones for freezing a suspicious site.

    (d) Nuclear material safeguards (based on bolstered IAEA safeguards of
        INFCIRC/540) are extended to all states.

    (e) IAEA recommendations for physical protection—as against theft or
        diversion—of nuclear material (INFCIRC/225/Rev. 4, or any pretreaty
        sequel) are mandatory under the treaty for all states.

    (f) Guarding of fissionable material while in transit is undertaken by con-
        tingents of an international, probably U.N.-affiliated Nuclear Protective
        Force (to provide security against a terrorist assault and to provide
        notice to the world at large in the event a shipment fell prey to seizure
        by a state's forces).

    (g) Treaty permanent council members are entitled to maintain observation
        and video surveillance or communication posts outside of states' sites
        holding separated plutonium (or HEU during its blending down).

14. (a) World stocks of HEU are blended down to LEU over a span of years.
       The time span may be lengthier than the weapons-elimination period,
       depending on how much current HEU (such as with the now past-mid-
       course 20-year purchase of 500 tons of Russian LEU blended down
       from HEU) is converted to LEU or consumed in reactors before nuclear
       ban declarations are submitted by states.

    (b) HEU use in reactors (predominantly naval and research) must cease six
        months before weapons elimination ends, with an exception thereafter
        for any highly protected HEU research projects approved by three-
        quarters executive council vote, including all permanent council mem-
        bers' votes.

15. To meet a specific NEO threat, permission may be granted by the executive
    council for strictly limited, internationally monitored production and use of
    nuclear explosion technology.

16. The nuclear ban treaty is of unlimited duration and declares that the prohibi-
    tion of nuclear weapons and of undeclared, unsafeguarded nuclear material
    and facilities applies everywhere.

17. The treaty Preamble warns and puts on notice all "new and future states"
    that they must abide by the treaty's prohibition of nuclear weapons and must
    promptly accede to the treaty.

Probably the most tradition-upending element of the treaty is nonwithdrawal.
The mitigating factor, as discussed in chapter 4 and noted in number 11 above,
is that states under Article 60(2) of the Vienna Convention on the Law of

treaties could temporarily cease their compliance with the nuclear ban's provisions if another state initially engaged in significant, willful treaty violation (i.e., material breach).

Another factor, noted in number 1, is that within 60 days after the U.N. Secretary-General announces achievement of unanimous accession by states to the treaty, any state could delay (without limitation of time) the treaty's entry into force. Doing so would cause a great international outcry unless a chaotic, ungoverned area somewhere posed a plausible nuclear threat, which is highly unlikely in a world in which all bona fide states have joined the nuclear ban.

Furthermore, as noted in number 5(b), any state could delay commencement of actual weapons elimination under the enacted treaty by voting that another state's domestic implementing legislation is "not acceptable." This, too, as with a vote to delay entry into force, would spark relentless criticism if there was no solid reason for the delay; and if there was solid reason, massive criticism would be directed against a state that, for example, was asserting in its implementing legislation a "national security exception" to treaty-authorized inspection.

Potent and overarching reasons would deter states from embarking on a course of treaty violation. First, each state according to its constitutional processes joined the treaty and thereby publicly accepted the obligations of the treaty, once all states have joined and it has entered into force. Second, any move to violate the treaty almost certainly would incite opposition even from within the state's leadership, because (unlike the current NPT) the ban treats states equally by prohibiting nuclear weapons to all. Third, the treaty's official verification regime, including challenge inspections initiated by individual states, would pose a major risk of exposure and thereby serve as a deterrent to any move toward treaty cheating. Fourth, a credible revelatory report of non-compliance by just one actor or citizen would attract the attention of the nuclear ban's executive council or technical secretariat, and, if warranted, special inspection. Fifth, the inducement to "whistle-blowing" of reward funds would further deter, through awareness of increased risk of exposure, any attempt to covertly violate the treaty. Sixth, states could not avoid foreseeing that a treaty-violating state would become (at a minimum) the political foe of the world's other states, currently numbering 194. Seventh, and not least, compliance with a nuclear ban treaty is manifestly necessary for humanity to reap its benefits of freedom from nuclear war, freedom from false-alarm nuclear strike, virtual elimination of the risk of nuclear terrorism (see below), and worldwide prohibition of chem-bio weapons through a requirement of accession by states to the CWC and BWC before signing the nuclear treaty.

George W. Bush has said, "Terror and weapons of mass destruction go hand in hand. To the extent that the free world can convince other nations to join together and rid the world of mass destruction weapons, we've done our children and grandchildren a great service."[1]

Lending solemn ear to this, the proposed nuclear ban treaty's barriers to mass destruction terrorism bear summary. First, with every state having renounced nuclear and chem-bio weapons, even some terrorists might develop second thoughts about attempting to attain and utilize the unanimously rejected instruments. Second, some terrorists may be more likely to refrain in the face of greater probability that a "harboring" state would rethink the matter and apprehend the terrorists (because consequences against a harboring state would be severe, with the three classes of weapons of mass destruction banned worldwide). Third, requirement of penal provision in states' implementing legislation may give pause to some terrorists—most of whom presumably wish to avoid incarceration, even if a fringe group is suicidal. Fourth, no CWC-prohibited chemicals nor weaponized biological agents would be stockpiled by states and be vulnerable to theft by or diversion to terrorists. Fifth, and most important, states would have no nuclear weapons that could be stolen or otherwise acquired by terrorists, and the blending down of HEU to LEU would eliminate the material for fabrication by terrorists of a relatively simple (and thus achievable) gun-type nuclear weapon.

Penultimately, some readers (including governmental leaders) may be asked whether they "agree" with the theme of this work—that worldwide prohibition of nuclear (and chem-bio) weapons can be achieved by treaty. Perhaps a prudent reply—particularly with respect to the perceived valid interests of a current nuclear weapon state—would be along this line:

> A world with no weapons of mass destruction, as unanimously agreed by states, would certainly be safer for all and protective of life. Therefore I support nuclear ban treaty creation, and I urge my country's serious participation in negotiations. However, I cannot promise my support or nonsupport for such a treaty until it is completed and formally introduced, so it can be examined in all its detail.

No inviolable barrier to proliferation or use of nuclear weapons currently exists, primarily because today's NPT is not unanimously joined, and the NPT permits withdrawal and does not prohibit nuclear weapons to the five pre-1967 possessors. A new, unanimously joined treaty banning nuclear weapons will be the culmination of the dedicated efforts of individuals, states, and organizations that has resulted in landmark agreements such as the NPT (1968), the partial (1963) and pending comprehensive test bans, the Intermediate-range Nuclear Forces Treaty (1987), START (1991), and the Moscow Treaty (2002).

In this age, the nuclear powers themselves are extremely concerned about proliferation and the possibility of nuclear weapons falling into terrorists' hands. A treaty banning nuclear weapons, and that requires signatories to be prior parties to the CWC and BWC, will enhance the present and future security of all people. We created these weapons and we can eliminate them, under fair and worldwide agreement.

Analysis of the Model Nuclear Weapons Convention

In April 1997 a 59-page Model Nuclear Weapons Convention (MNWC) was issued by the American affiliate of the International Association of Lawyers Against Nuclear Arms, the Lawyers' Committee on Nuclear Policy.[1] The purpose in drafting the Model Convention was to attempt to demonstrate the feasibility of a treaty banning nuclear weapons and to create an impetus for nuclear weapons ban negotiations by states, of which the International Court of Justice (the World Court) in a 1996 Advisory Opinion stated, "There exists an obligation to pursue in good faith and to bring to a conclusion negotiations leading to nuclear disarmament in all its aspects under strict and effective international control."[2] (This finding was predicated on today's Non-Proliferation Treaty (NPT), with its many worldwide signatory states and its various references to nuclear disarmament.)

Existence of the MNWC boosts the work of the international Abolition 2000 network.[3] The appellation "2000" remains in use, presumably for reasons of convenience and harking to the network's original (1995) goal that a nuclear weapons ban treaty, largely based on the then-prospective MNWC text, be opened for states' signatures by 2000.

The MNWC is an official U.N. discussion document (U.N. Doc. A/C.1/ 52.7). Creation of the Model Convention by its drafters—50 volunteer lawyers, engineers, scientists, physicians, and consultants—was motivated by desire to spare present and future humanity from the use of nuclear weapons (including prohibition of radiological weapons or "dirty bombs," which disperse radioactive material with conventional explosives).

The Model Convention's Preamble summarizes the rationale for elimination of nuclear weapons, including their indiscriminately destructive explosive power, their ongoing threat to life and security of person, environmental effects of their creation, the possibility of false-alarm nuclear war or terrorist acquisition of a bomb, the "medically and psychologically catastrophic effects of any use of nuclear weapons, the potential effects of mutation in the genetic pool," and the contrariness of nuclear weapons to humanitarian norms of international law.

Before treading the road of critique (which is much easier than creation), it bears emphasis that the MNWC is worthy of international respect—for several reasons. First, no other proposed treaty text has been created for the elimination of nuclear weapons. Second, the MNWC is well organized. Third, the bulk of its provisions—in 19 main sections—are unassailable for elimination and prohibition of nuclear weapons. Fourth, the Model Convention designedly leans heavily in overall structure and in various important provisions on extant agreements, particularly the long-negotiated Chemical Weapons Convention (CWC).

The MNWC ably covers much ground, some of it pro forma in modern treaties, which is not duplicated in *Banning Weapons of Mass Destruction*. Therefore, before any wholesale evaluation of "omissions" in this text, readers are respectfully asked to also examine the MNWC. (This text, however, has attempted to address formidable "lingering" questions and issues attendant on successfully banning nuclear weapons.)

A Verification Annex, establishing details of nuclear ban inspection, is *not* part of the MNWC, although basic duties of the technical secretariat such as conducting challenge inspections (as with the CWC) are set forth (please see chapter 5 of *Banning Weapons of Mass Destruction* for discussion of proposed inspection principles for a worldwide nuclear weapons ban).

This appendix comments further on recommendations, gleaned from the main body of *Banning Weapons of Mass Destruction*, for nuclear ban treaty provisions. All the provisions could be integrated into the MNWC—which was not illiberally set forth as unalterable in every aspect of its provisions. And, although the great majority of the MNWC's "unassailable" provisions (again, many based on skillful adaptation from the CWC and other treaties) are unmentioned and therefore unheralded in this analysis, the existence of the Model Convention will, due to its merits, probably save up to 80 percent of the time that otherwise would be necessary to draft a finalized nuclear ban treaty, ready for states' signatures. (Without most or all of the proposed treaty provisions recapitulated here, however, a nuclear ban treaty may not gain unanimous accession and enter into force.)

The mention of "unanimous accession" brings up the first point, namely, that accession by all the world's states is not required for the Model Convention's entry into force; rather, the pertinent provision includes all five NPT nuclear weapon states, plus nuclear powers that are not party to the NPT (Pakistan, India, North Korea, and Israel), plus states possessing a nuclear reactor, plus enough other states (about 20) to total 65—incidentally, the same total number required for CWC entry into force. However, with respect to nuclear weapons, even if a nonthreatening, smallish country (Country X) does not have to and does not join a nuclear ban before it enters into force, the United States and some other countries in all probability will not join, based on apprehension that Country X (or another nonsignatory) could in the future decide to develop nuclear weapons. Most countries in fact have long-renounced nuclear weapons by being non-nuclear weapon parties to the NPT, but the NPT permits states to withdraw. In any case, the NPT would be defunct when replaced by a new nuclear treaty. If Country X did actually undertake nuclear weapons development, then the United States and other countries would feel themselves hamstrung, given that they abjured nuclear weapons by joining the ban and did so without the participation of Country X. The vast majority of states today are not suspected of harboring intentions to develop nuclear weapons, but the current nuclear powers would insist that a nuclear ban be unanimously joined before it takes effect.

The Model Convention's provision for entry into force does indeed entail accession by today's five NPT nuclear weapon states, plus the four nuclear-capable states outside the NPT, and all states with a nuclear reactor (which produces plutonium). The Model Convention's exigent accession for entry into force by those particular states (plus others totaling 65) supports the feasibility of requiring accession by *all* states before nuclear ban entry into force, which again would be crucial for gaining accession by today's nuclear powers.

However, "all states" cannot simply be listed by name in the treaty as necessary, aggregate signatories for entry into force, because one or more "new states" could emerge after the treaty is opened for signature but before unanimous accession is achieved. Therefore, it is proposed that the U.N. Secretary-General be tasked or requested in the treaty to declare when, based on his or her judgment, "all states have joined." As discussed in chapter 3, this announcement by the Secretary-General marks the first one-third of a 180-day interval leading to entry into force, and during the first 60 days any state is entitled to object to entry into force and thereby rescind the commenced 180-day interval, and with a new such interval (with a new 60-day window for objection) commencing whenever the objection is withdrawn. This provision will act to neutralize any consequential concern on the part of states that the Secretary-General might issue a "premature" announcement that "all states" have joined. The nuclear ban, though, upon unanimous accession when in all probability so announced by the Secretary-General, would have such momentum that it is unlikely that a state would choose to anger the world by delaying entry into force for a factitious reason.

It is also key that before submission of treaty-required nuclear declarations takes place, all states enact domestic implementing legislation that is held by consensus of states to be "acceptable" (sufficient in scope and noncontradictory to the treaty). Absent this provision, some states would not sign the treaty, under the mantle of worry that one or more other states might lay claim to "national security exception" to inspection or assert other solipsistic treaty contradiction in domestic implementing legislation.

Also before actual weapons elimination begins, it is proposed that nuclear ban parties must vote without demurral that the treaty process should proceed to the next step. This vote, taken after nuclear declarations by states have been submitted and their verification undertaken and completed by the technical secretariat, would be a referendum by all states on their fellow states' compliance (or lack thereof) with treaty-required declarations and cooperation in their verification. Therefore, the start of weapons elimination could be delayed (theoretically indefinitely) by one negative vote, just as one negative vote concerning acceptability of a state or states' implementing legislation would delay states' submissions of nuclear declarations until the objection is withdrawn. However, the satisfactoriness of implementing legislation, and of declarations and cooperation in their verification, are the two critical areas, along with whether "all states" have joined with respect to which many states will insist on holding "veto power"—over treaty entry into force, submission of declarations, and commencement of weapons elimination. Again, though, a *unanimously joined* treaty's geopolitical momentum would push all states toward full compliance and thereby reduce any chance that a state would feel the need to delay any of those important steps of treaty actualization.

Continuing, the MNWC does not absolve its signatory states of the obligation under Article 18(a) of the Vienna Convention the Law of Treaties to refrain from defeating a treaty's "object and purpose" after signing or ratifying but before the treaty by its terms officially enters into force. A nuclear weapons ban needs to provide an exemption from this basic element of international treaty law, or the current nuclear powers likely will refuse to sign and ratify it; those states only will oblige themselves to adhere to the fundamental object and purpose of such a ban (i.e., nonuse of the weapons) simultaneously with all states. The Law of Treaties' "object and purpose" stricture is salubrious regarding treaties in general, but not for a nuclear ban treaty. (It is to the credit of humanity that all but nine state are now non-nuclear weapon parties to the 1968 NPT, and the NPT as emphasized would still be in force during accumulation of nuclear ban signatories.)

Next, the MNWC does not mandate prior accession by states to the current chemical and biological weapons bans as a prerequisite for signing the MNWC. Yet, if considered to be the foundation to successfully rid the world of nuclear weapons, it is realistic to expect that states would agree to renounce chem-bio weapons by acceding to the 1993 CWC and 1972 BWC before signing a nuclear ban (see discussion in chapter 9). Moreover, at least some of the many countries that have joined the CWC and BWC predictably would refuse to join the nuclear ban if other countries could with relative ease and a guise of impunity (being nonsignatories of the CWC and/or BWC) develop chemical or biological, or both such repellent weapons. Elimination of nuclear weapons must be made as welcome as possible to the nuclear weapon states, and a wind of inducement to join will be the requirement of accession by states to the bans on chem-bio weapons before signing the nuclear ban treaty.

The major reason the MNWC does not mandate accession by states to the CWC and BWC before signing the nuclear ban is that the ultimate weapons of mass destruction are nuclear weapons—they being easily delivered and more reliably, variously (blast, heat, radiation, fires), and widely lethal than other contrivances. But it is to be expected that today's nuclear weapon states will insist that elimination of nuclear arms be preceded by formal renunciation (through CWC and BWC accession) by all states of justly abhorred chemical and biological weapons.

Next, on the issue of withdrawal, the MNWC prohibits it, and this is logical due to the positive import of elimination of nuclear weapons and the instability if states could "at the drop of a hat" (so to speak) *legally* withdraw or threaten to withdraw. But, to be acceptable to all states, it is nearly certain that a non-withdrawal nuclear ban treaty also needs the following related elements: (1) an acknowledgment, at least indirectly, that material breach by a state would allow (under the Vienna Convention on the Law of Treaties) another state or states to *temporarily* disregard the ban; (2) provision that a state or states "responding" to a material breach by another state must publicly name the treaty-violating state before disregarding the treaty (and to avoid world outrage would need to present sufficient evidence to credit the charge); and (3) provision that the responding state or states are obliged in good faith to publicly announce when they deem the initially violating state to no longer be in material breach, after which announcement by the responding state (or the final one of them, if several), those states must recomply with the treaty, including internationally monitored dismantling of any newly created nuclear weapons within 30 days.

The MNWC stipulates in Article IV(D), "Phases for Implementation," that by two years after entry into force, "All warheads shall be removed from their delivery vehicles and either placed into internationally monitored storage facilities or dismantled." This storage or dismantling of warheads—within just two years—could possibly be structured and undertaken to the satisfaction of today's nuclear power, but so rapid a step of this breadth will be problematic if it is not tailored to thoroughly answer any remotely reasonable security concerns of states. The alternative approach (which may be necessary, given world realities) is to progressively dismantle all nuclear warheads within a time-bound framework and under mandatory declarations, while *allowing the diminishing number of warheads to continue to exist as weapons for almost the entirety of the weapons-elimination period* (until dismantling of residual arsenals of states during the final four or so weeks).

In nuclear ban negotiations, if the current nuclear weapon states cannot be convinced that disabling and internationally monitoring the storage of all warheads while awaiting dismantling is feasible from the security standpoint, then that contention should not upset the prospects for banning nuclear weapons. *Without* such disabling and monitored storage, nuclear weapons would still be ready for use, but in steadily diminishing numbers under the time-bound framework of the treaty's elimination period. It would be extremely regrettable if a prospective nuclear weapons ban should flounder on the issue of whether internationally monitored storage, or outright dismantling, must be so quickly accomplished. If for their part, however, the United States and Russia only possessed nuclear arsenals comparable to those of China, France, or Britain, then the gradual, prudent dismantling of the world's nuclear warheads could be accomplished in a year or less. Also, even though it may well be decided (in nuclear ban negotiations) that diminishing numbers of nuclear weapons must be able to remain ready for immediate use (not stored under monitoring) until the end of the elimination period, the treaty when it simply enters into force contains states' pledge *not to use* nuclear weapons. Legally speaking, on the chance a state *did* assault another with nuclear weapons during the weapons-elimination period, that would be an ultimate material breach of the ban and would legally liberate the target state, or even its ally, to respond in kind. Certainly, though, as a nuclear ban is finalized, introduced, accumulates signatories, and enters into force, worldwide disapproval of use or possible use of nuclear weapons will grow ever stronger.

It would also be appropriate for the duration of the weapons-elimination period (such as three, four, or five years) to be set by a treaty-specified scale according to the higher remaining number of U.S. or Russian warheads at the time, after baseline verification of states' nuclear declarations is completed, that all treaty parties agree that the treaty process should proceed to the next step. Otherwise, the treaty might stipulate longer than necessary for elimination of warheads, specifically if reductions have been ongoing or are accelerated, perhaps for reasons apart from the prospective nuclear ban, by the United States and Russia after the ban is introduced but before achievement of unanimous accession and entry into force. Also, it maybe judged a workable compromise that all nuclear powers except the United States and Russia must dismantle 25 percent of their warheads within the first three months of the elimination period, and the former states thereafter need not proceed with weapons dismantling until the U.S. and Russian arsenals have decreased (following the treaty timetable) to the other states' respective new, lower levels. So, during *most* of the elimination period, the United States and Russia would still have a large majority of the world's nuclear weapons; but over the span of the final 12 months, the U.S.-Russian reductions would bring their warhead totals down to the varying, respective levels of the other nuclear powers (culminating on the same day when all must reach zero).

MNWC Article XII stipulates:

> Each State party shall adopt the necessary measures to ensure that [weapons and] weapons delivery systems are only developed, produced, otherwise acquired, retained, transferred, tested or deployed in a manner consistent with this Convention. To this end, and in order to verify that activities are in accordance with obligations under this Convention, *each State party shall subject weapons delivery system, including command, communication, control and production facilities ... to verification measures*" (emphasis added).

The bracketing of "weapons and" indicates a tentative MNWC recommendation. Whether such a provision would encompass only "weapons delivery systems" or also "weapons," it is most likely too intrusive in states' military matters. The main objective would be to detect (and deter through monitoring) the development and possession of delivery systems designed for nuclear weapons; but nuclear warheads can be carried by some regular bombers, or smuggled in trucks or ships, so the above measure even if acceptable to all states would not free people from the means to deliver nuclear weapons.

If evidence was presented to the treaty regime that Country X was fabricating nuclear warheads at a hidden site, or concealing a stock of plutonium or enriched uranium, then that would merit nuclear ban inquiry and, if necessary, special inspection. It is too much, though, to ask the world's states under nuclear ban auspices to subject to ongoing verification measures "[weapons and] weapons delivery systems, including command, communication, control and production facilities."

Next, the MNWC does not prohibit nuclear power with LEU fuel but does ban plutonium reprocessing. This is an arguable recommendation for a nuclear weapons ban, because reprocessing centers on plutonium separated from irradiated reactor fuel, and plutonium (and HEU) are the prime materials for nuclear weapons. But prohibition of reprocessing would likely be unacceptable to a few states at least—because the treaty is of indefinite duration and does not permit withdrawal, and the earth has only a finite supply of uranium for LEU fuel use in power reactors (on the "once-through" basis, without reprocessing to separate plutonium for use as a component of new reactor fuel). Therefore it is submitted that reprocessing should not be prohibited, or the treaty likely would never achieve unanimity and enter into force.

Second, the MNWC mandates elimination of intercontinental and submarine-launched ballistic missiles, ballistic missile submarines, heavy bombers, ground-launched cruise missile, plus elimination or conversion to non-nuclear capability of air-to-surface missiles, ground-launched and sea-launched cruise missiles, nuclear-capable fighter-bombers, attack submarines, and warships. With today's compact nuclear warheads, many if not most delivery systems could not be converted to certifiably non-nuclear use—and one can only view as unlikely that the United States would destroy its heavy bombers under a nuclear ban treaty. Liberation from nuclear weapons does not require dismantling or conversion (if even possible) to genuinely non-nuclear use of the world's advanced weapons delivery systems; rather, the pivotal requirement is unanimity of states' accession to a nuclear ban, and with the incentive to join of no treaty-related obligations on states until all have joined and entry into force is attained (but with today's NPT remaining in effect for its parties until nuclear ban entry into force).

The nuclear ban treaty should indicate the will of all states that "future states" must never develop nuclear weapons and must promptly join the treaty—preceded, as with extant states, by accession to the CWC and BWC. And, the treaty's nonwithdrawal provision gives need of a declaration that the prohibition of nuclear weapons is applicable everywhere, to ensure that a breakaway state or area could not claim, without incurring worldwide opposition, to be outside the treaty's reach. (See chapter 14 for summary of all major suggested treaty provisions.)

This appendix's recitation of suggested emendations to the MNWC is perhaps misleading as to its value, because largely unsaid are the MNWC's imperturbable sections and provisions (including but not limited to those felicitously adapted for nuclear weapons from agreements such as the CWC). When states undertake actual negotiation of a nuclear weapons ban, the MNWC will fulfill its destined role as a vital, time-saving, largely foundational initial "rolling text." Meanwhile, the treaty provisions and other discussion in *Banning Weapons of Mass Destruction* hopefully will hasten the day of worldwide liberation from nuclear and chem-bio weapons.

1968 Non-Proliferation Treaty

The Non-Proliferation Treaty (NPT), today's "global" nuclear arms control regime, required 43 parties for entry into force. The treaty was first signed at Washington, D.C., Moscow, and London on July 1, 1968, and entered into force for its parties on March 5, 1970.

Central to the treaty is its provision that NPT non-nuclear weapon states must conclude nuclear material safeguards agreements with the International Atomic Energy Agency (Article III). Among NPT elements *excluded* from the proposed nuclear ban treaty are the undertaking of parties to facilitate the fullest possible exchange of technological information, and so on, for peaceful uses of nuclear energy (Article IV); a provision earmarking nuclear weapon states (Article IX); and permitted withdrawal (Article X).

Also excluded is an NPT-type injunction for sharing between states "potential benefits from any peaceful applications of nuclear explosions" (Article V). The nuclear ban's executive council could authorize production of internationally monitored "nuclear explosive devices" to counter a clear and present Near-Earth Object danger, but not for excavation or other conceivable purpose.

As adumbrated in Article X, the NPT was "extended indefinitely" in 1995; but the NPT would be superseded, under principles of the Vienna Convention on the Law of Treaties, by a worldwide nuclear ban treaty when it enters into force.

TREATY ON THE NON-PROLIFERATION OF NUCLEAR WEAPONS

The States concluding this Treaty, hereinafter referred to as the "Parties to the Treaty,"

Considering the devastation that would be visited upon all mankind by a nuclear war and the consequent need to make every effort to avert the danger of such a war and to take measures to safeguard the security of peoples,

Believing that the proliferation of nuclear weapons would seriously enhance the danger of nuclear wear,

In conformity with the resolutions of the United Nations General Assembly calling for conclusion of an agreement on the prevention of wider dissemination of nuclear weapons,

Undertaking to cooperate in facilitating the application of International Atomic Energy Agency safeguards on peaceful nuclear activities,

Expressing their support for research, development and other efforts to further the application, within the framework of the International Atomic Energy safeguards system, of the principle of safeguarding effectively the flow of source and special fissionable materials by use of instruments and other techniques at certain strategic points,

Affirming the principle that the benefits of peaceful applications of nuclear technology, including any technological by-products which may be derived by nuclear-weapon States from the development of nuclear explosive devices, should be available for peaceful purposes to all Parties of the Treaty, whether nuclear weapon or non-nuclear weapon States,

Convinced that, in furtherance of this principle, all Parties to the Treaty are entitled to participate in the fullest possible exchange of scientific information for, and to contribute alone or in cooperation with other States to, the further development of the applications of atomic energy for peaceful purposes,

Declaring their intention to achieve at the earliest possible date the cessation of the nuclear arms race and to undertake effective measures in the direction of nuclear disarmament,

Urging the cooperation of all States in the attainment of this objective,

Recalling the determination expressed by the Parties to the 1963 Treaty banning nuclear weapons tests in the atmosphere, in outer space and under water in its preamble to seek to achieve the discontinuance of all test explosions of nuclear weapons for all time and to continue negotiations to this end,

Desiring to further the easing of international tension and the strengthening of trust between States in order to facilitate the cessation of the manufacture of nuclear weapons, the liquidation of existing stockpiles, and the elimination from national arsenals of nuclear weapons and the means of their deliver pursuant to a treaty on general and complete disarmament under strict and effective international control,

Recalling that, in accordance with the Charter of the United Nations, States must refrain in their international relations from the threat or use of force against the territorial integrity or political independence of any State, or in any other manner inconsistent with the purposes of the United Nations, and that the establishment and maintenance of international peace and security are to be promoted with the least diversion of armaments of the world's human and economic resource,

Have agreed as follows,

Article I

Each nuclear weapon State Party to the Treaty undertakes not to transfer to any recipient whatsoever nuclear weapons or other nuclear explosive devices or control over such weapons or explosive devices either directly, or indirectly; and not in any way to otherwise acquire nuclear weapons or other nuclear explosive devices, or control over such weapons or explosive devices.

Article II

Each non-nuclear weapon State Party to the Treaty undertakes not to receive the transfer from any transfer or whatsoever of nuclear weapons or other nuclear explosive devices or of control over such weapons or explosive devices directly, or indirectly; not to manufacture or otherwise acquire nuclear weapons or other nuclear explosive devices; and not to seek or receive any assistance in the manufacture of nuclear weapons or other nuclear explosive devices.

Article III

1. Each non-nuclear weapon State Party to the Treaty undertakes to accept safeguards, as set forth in an agreement to be negotiated and concluded with the International Atomic Energy Agency in accordance with the Statute of the International Atomic Energy Agency and the Agency's safeguards system, for the exclusive purpose of verification of the fulfillment of its obligations assumed under this Treaty with a view to preventing diversion of nuclear energy from peaceful uses to nuclear weapons or other nuclear explosive devices. Procedures for the safeguards required by this Article shall be followed with respect to source or special fissionable material whether it is being produced, processed or used in any principal nuclear facility or is outside any such facility. The safeguards required by this Article shall be applied to all source or special fissionable material in all peaceful nuclear activities within the territory of such State, under its jurisdiction, or carried out under its control anywhere.

2. Each State Party to the Treaty undertakes not to provide: (a) source or special fissionable material, or (b) equipment or material designed or prepared for the processing, use or production of special fissionable material, to any non-nuclear weapon State for peaceful purposes, unless the source or special fissionable material shall be subject to safeguards required by this Article.

3. The safeguards required by this Article shall be implemented in a manner designed to comply with Article IV of this Treaty, and to avoid hampering the economic or technological development of the Parties or international cooperation in the field of peaceful nuclear activities, including the international exchange of nuclear material for peaceful purposes in accordance with the provisions of this Article and the principle of safeguarding set forth in the Preamble of the Treaty.

4. Non-nuclear weapon States Party to the Treaty shall conclude agreements with the International Atomic Energy Agency to meet the requirements of this Article either individually or together with other States in accordance with the Statute of the International Atomic Energy Agency. Negotiation of such agreements shall commence within 180 days from the original entry into force of this Treaty. For States depositing their instruments of ratification or accession after the 180-day period, negotiations of such agreements shall commence not later than the date of such deposit. Such agreements

shall enter into force no later than eighteen months after the date of initiation of negotiations.

Article IV

1. Nothing in this Treaty shall be interpreted as affecting the inalienable right of all Parties to the Treaty to development, research, production and use of nuclear energy for peaceful purposes without discrimination and in conformity with Articles I and II of this Treaty.
2. All the Parties to the Treaty undertake to facilitate, and have the right to participate in, the fullest possible exchange of equipment, materials and scientific and technological information for the peaceful uses of nuclear energy. Parties to the Treaty in a position to do so shall also cooperate in contributing alone or together with other States or international organizations to the further development of the applications of nuclear energy for peaceful purposes, especially in the territories of non-nuclear weapon States Party to the Treaty, with due consideration for the needs of the developing areas of the world.

Article V

Each Party to the Treaty undertakes to take appropriate measures to ensure that, in accordance with this Treaty, under appropriate international observation and through appropriate international procedures, potential benefits from any peaceful applications of nuclear explosions will be made available to non-nuclear weapon States Party to the Treaty on a nondiscriminatory basis and that the charge to such Parties for the explosive devices used will be as low as possible and exclude any charge for research and development. Non-nuclear weapon State Party to the Treaty shall be able to obtain such benefits, pursuant to a special international agreement or agreements, through an appropriate international body with adequate representation of non-nuclear weapon States. Negotiations on this subject shall commence as soon as possible after the Treaty enters into force. Non-nuclear weapon States Party to the Treaty so desiring may also obtain such benefits pursuant to bilateral agreements.

Article VI

Each of the Parties to the Treaty undertakes to pursue negotiations in good faith on effective measures relating to cessation of the nuclear arms race at an early date and to nuclear disarmament, and on a treaty on general and complete disarmament under strict and effective international control.

Article VII

Nothing in this Treaty affects the right of any group of States to conclude regional treaties in order to assure the total absence of nuclear weapons in their respective territories.

Article VIII

1. Any Party to the Treaty may propose amendments to this Treaty. The text of any proposed amendment shall be submitted to the Depositary Governments,

which shall circulate it to all Parties to the Treaty. Thereupon, if requested to do so by one-third or more of the Parties to the Treaty, the Depositary governments shall convene a conference, to which they shall invite all the Parties to the Treaty, to consider such an amendment.

2. Any amendment to the Treaty must be approved by a majority of the votes of all Parties to the Treaty, including the votes of all nuclear weapon States Party to the Treaty and all other Parties which, on the date the amendment is circulated, are members of the Board of Governors of the International Atomic Energy Agency. The amendment shall enter into force for each Party that deposits its instruments of ratification of the amendment upon the deposit of such instruments of ratification by a majority of all the Parties, including the instruments of ratification of all nuclear weapon States Party to the Treaty and all other Parties which, on the date the amendment is circulated, are members of the Board of Governors of the International Atomic Energy Agency. Thereafter, it shall enter into force for any other Party upon the deposit of its instruments of ratification of the amendments.

3. Five years after the entry into force of this Treaty, a conference of Parties to the Treaty shall be held in Geneva, Switzerland, in order to review the operation of this Treaty, with a view to assuring that that purposes of the Preamble and provisions of the Treaty are being realized. At intervals of five years thereafter, a majority of the Parties to the Treaty may obtain, by submitting a proposal to this effect to the Depositary Governments, the convening of further conferences with the same objective of reviewing the operation of the Treaty.

Article IX

1. This Treaty shall be open to all States for signature. Any State which does not sign the Treaty before its entry into force in accordance with paragraph 3 of this Article may accede to it at any time.

2. This Treaty shall be subject to ratification by signatory States. Instruments of ratification and instruments of accession shall be deposited with the Governments of the United States of America, the United Kingdom of Great Britain and Northern Ireland and the Union of Soviet Socialist Republics, which are hereby designated the Depositary Governments.

3. This Treaty shall enter into force after its ratification by the States, the Governments of which are designated Depositaries of the Treaty, and forty other States signatory to this Treaty and the deposit of their instruments of ratification. For the purposes of this Treaty, a nuclear weapon State is one which has manufactured and exploded a nuclear weapon or other nuclear explosive device prior to January 1, 1967.

4. For States whose instruments of ratification or accession are deposited subsequently to the entry into force of this Treaty, it shall enter into force on the date of the deposit of their instruments of ratification or accession.

5. The Depositary Governments shall promptly inform all signatory and acceding States of the date of each signature, the date of deposit of each deposit of instrument of ratification or of accession, the date of the entry into force of this Treaty, and the date of receipt of any request for convening a conference or other notices.

Article X

1. Each Party shall in exercising its national sovereignty have the right to withdraw from the Treaty if it decides that extraordinary events, related to the subject-matter of this Treaty, have jeopardized the supreme interests of its country. It shall give notice of such withdrawal to all other Parties to the Treaty and to the United Nations Security Council three months in advance. Such notice shall include a statement of the extraordinary events it regards as having jeopardized its supreme interests.

2. Twenty-five years after the entry into force of the Treaty, a conference shall be convened to decide whether the Treaty shall continue in force indefinitely, or shall be extended for an additional fixed period or periods. This decision shall be taken by a majority of the Parties to the Treaty.

Article XI

This treaty, the English, Russian, French, Spanish and Chinese texts of which are equally authentic, shall be deposited in the archives of the Depositary Governments. Duly certified copies of this Treaty shall be transmitted by the Depositary Governments to the Governments of the signatory and acceding States.

In witness the undersigned, duly authorized, have signed this Treaty.

Done in triplicate, at the cities of Washington, London, and Moscow, this first day of July one thousand nine hundred sixty-eight.

1972 Biological Weapons Convention

The 1925 Geneva Protocol prohibited to its signatory states the use against each other of chemical and bacteriological (biological) methods of warfare, but production and stockpiling of chem-bio weapons was not banned. During the Cold War, U.S.-Soviet discussions on biological weapons were periodically undertaken, and on November 11, 1969, President Nixon announced that the United States was renouncing biological weapons (and "first use" of chemical weapons).

The Soviet Union had long argued that chemical and biological weapons should be prohibited by a single treaty, but in 1971 the Soviets submitted a draft agreement dealing only with biological and related "toxin" weapons. Ensuing negotiations culminated in a Biological Weapons Convention (BWC) that entered into force (for its parties) on March 26, 1975, with accumulation of required 22 parties; now some 83 percent of states are full BWC parties, and of nonratified signatories and nonsignatories, most are not suspected of possession of bioweapon arsenals.

In line with treaties in general, the BWC permits withdrawal; however, under the proposed nuclear ban treaty, states relinquish their right to BWC (and Chemical Weapons Convention [CWC]) withdrawal once the nuclear ban attains unanimity and enters into force.

CONVENTION ON THE PROHIBITION OF THE DEVELOPMENT, PRODUCTION, AND STOCKPILING OF BACTERIOLOGICAL (BIOLOGICAL) AND TOXIN WEAPONS AND ON THEIR DESTRUCTION

The States Parties to this Convention,

Determined to act with a view to achieving effective progress towards general and complete disarmament, including the prohibition and elimination of all types of weapons of mass destruction, and convinced that the prohibition of the development, production and stockpiling of chemical and bacteriological (biological) weapons and their elimination, through effective measures, will facilitate the achievement of general and complete disarmament under strict and effective international control,

Recognizing the important significance of the Protocol for the Prohibition of the Use in War of Asphyxiating, Poisonous or Other Gases, and of Bacteriological Methods of Warfare, signed at Geneva on June 17, 1925, and conscious also of the contribution which the said Protocol has already made, and continues to make, to mitigate the horrors of war,

Reaffirming their adherence to the principles and objectives of the Protocol and calling upon all States to comply strictly with them,

Recalling that the General Assembly of the United Nations has repeatedly condemned all actions contrary to the principles and objectives of the Geneva Protocol of June 17, 1925,

Desiring to contribute to the strengthening of confidence between peoples and general improvement of the international atmosphere,

Desiring also to contribute to the realization of the purposes and principles of the Charter of the United Nations,

Convinced of the importance and urgency of eliminating from the arsenals of States, through effective measures, such dangerous weapons of mass destruction as those using chemical or bacteriological (biological) agents,

Recognizing that an agreement on the prohibition of bacteriological (biological) and toxin weapons represents a first possible step towards the achievement of agreement on effective measures also for the prohibition of the development, production and stockpiling of chemical weapons, and determined to continue negotiations to that end,

Determined, for the sake of mankind, to exclude completely the possibility of bacteriological (biological) agents and toxins being used as weapons,

Convinced that such use would be repugnant to the conscience of mankind and that no effort should be spared to minimize this risk,

Have agreed as follows:

Article I
Each State Party to this Convention undertakes never in any circumstances to develop, produce, stockpile or otherwise retain:

(1) Microbial and other biological agents, or toxins whatever their origin or method of production, of types and in quantities that have no justification for prophylactic, protective or other peaceful purposes;
(2) Weapons, equipment or means of delivery designed to use such agents or toxins for hostile purposes or in armed conflict.

Article II
Each State Party to this Convention undertakes to destroy, or to divert to peaceful purposes, as soon as possible but not later than nine months after the entry into force of this Convention, all agents, toxins, weapons, equipment and means of delivery specified in Article 1 of the Convention, which are in its possession or under its jurisdiction or control. In implementing the provision of this Article all necessary safety precautions shall be observed to protect populations and the environment.

Article III

Each State Party to this Convention undertakes not to transfer to any recipient whatsoever, directly or indirectly, and not in any way to assist, encourage, or induce any State, group of States or international organizations to manufacture or otherwise acquire any of the agents, toxins, weapons, equipment or means of delivery specified in Article 1 of the Convention.

Article IV

Each State Party to this Convention shall, in accordance with its constitutional processes, take any necessary measures to prohibit and prevent the development, production, stockpiling, acquisition, or retention of the agents, toxins, weapons, equipment and means of delivery specified in Article 1 of the Convention, within the territory of such State, under its jurisdiction or under its control anywhere.

Article V

The States parties to this Convention undertake to consult one another and to cooperate in solving any problems which may arise in relation to the objective of, or in the application of the provisions of, the Convention. Consultation and cooperation pursuant to this Article may also be undertaken through appropriate international procedures within the framework of the United Nations and in accordance with its Charter.

Article VI

(1) Any State Party to this Convention which finds that any other State Party is acting in breach of obligations deriving from the provisions of the Convention may lodge a complaint with the Security Council of the United Nations. Such a complaint should include all possible evidence confirming its validity, as well as a request for its consideration by the Security Council.

(2) Each State Party to this Convention undertakes to cooperate in carrying out any investigation which the Security Council may initiate, in accordance with the provisions of the Charter of the United Nations, on the basis of the complaint received by the Council. The Security Council shall inform the States Parties to the Convention of the results of the investigation.

Article VII

Each State party to this Convention undertakes to provide or support assistance, in accordance with the United Nations Charter, to any Party to the Convention which so requests, if the Security Council decides that such Party has been exposed to danger as a result of violation of this Convention.

Article VIII

Nothing in this Convention shall be interpreted as in any way limiting or detracting from the obligations assumed by States under the Protocol for the Prohibition of the Use in War of Asphyxiating, Poisonous or Other Gases, and of Bacteriological Methods of Warfare, signed at Geneva on June 17, 1925.

Article IX

Each State Party to this Convention affirms the recognized objective of effective prohibition of chemical weapons and, to this end, undertakes to continue negotiations in good faith with a view to reaching early agreement on effective measures for the prohibition of their development, production and stockpiling and for their destruction, and on appropriate measures concerning equipment and means of delivery specifically designed for the production or use of chemical agents for weapons purposes.

Article X

(1) The States Parties of this Convention undertake to facilitate, and have the right to participate in, the fullest possible exchange of equipment, materials and scientific and technological information for the use of bacteriological (biological) agents and toxins for peaceful purposes. Parties to the Convention in a position to do so shall also cooperate in contributing individually or together with other States or international organizations to the further development and application of scientific discoveries in the field of bacteriology (biology) for prevention of disease, or for other peaceful purpose.

(2) This Convention shall be implemented in a manner designed to avoid hampering the economic or technological development by States Parties to the Convention or international cooperation in the field of peaceful bacteriological (biological) activities, including the international exchange of bacteriological (biological) agents and toxins for peaceful purposes in accordance with the provisions of this Convention.

Article XI

Any State Party may propose amendments to the Convention. Amendments shall enter into force for each State Party accepting the amendments upon their acceptance by a majority of the States Parties to the Convention and thereafter for each remaining State Party on the date of acceptance by it.

Article XII

Five years after the entry into force of this Convention, or earlier if it is requested by a majority of Parties to the Convention by submitting a proposal to this effect to the Depositary Governments, a conference of States Parties to the Convention shall be held at Geneva, Switzerland, to review the operation of the Convention, with a view to assuring that the purposes of the Preamble and the provisions of the Convention, including the provisions concerning negotiations on chemical weapons, are being realized. Such review shall take into account any new scientific and technological developments relevant to the Convention.

Article XIII

(1) This Convention shall be of unlimited duration.

(2) Each State Party to this Convention shall in exercising its national sovereignty have the right to withdraw from the Convention if it decides that extraordinary events, related to the subject-matter of the Convention, have jeopardized its supreme interests. It shall give notice of such withdrawal to all other States Parties to the Convention and to the United Nations Security Council three months in advance. Such notice shall include a statement of the extraordinary events that it regards as having jeopardized its supreme interests.

Article XIV

(1) This Convention shall be open to all States for signature. Any State which does not sign the Convention before its entry into force in accordance with paragraph (3) of this Article may accede to it at any time.

(2) This Convention shall be subject to ratification by signatory States. Instruments of ratification and instruments of accession shall be deposited with the Governments of the United States of America, the United Kingdom of Great Britain and Northern Ireland and the Union of Soviet Socialist Republics, which are hereby designated as the Depositary Governments.

(3) The Convention shall enter into force after the deposit of instruments of ratification by twenty-two governments, including the Governments designated as Depositaries for the Convention.

(4) For States whose instruments of ratification or accession are deposited subsequent to the entry into force of this Convention, it shall enter into force on the date of the deposit of their instruments of ratification or accession.

(5) The Depositary Governments shall promptly inform all signatory and acceding States of the date of each signature, the date of deposit of each instrument of ratification or accession of accession and the date of the entry into force of this Convention, and of the receipt of other notices.

(6) This Convention shall be registered by the Depositary Governments pursuant to Article 102 of the Charter of the United Nations.

Article XV

This Convention, the English, Russian, French, Spanish and Chinese text of which are equally authentic, shall be deposited in the archives of the Depositary Governments. Duly certified copies of the Convention shall be transmitted by the Depositary Governments to the Governments of the signatory and acceding States.

IN WITNESS WHEREOF the undersigned, duly authorized, have signed this Convention.

DONE in triplicate, at the cities of Washington, London and Moscow, this tenth date of April, one thousand nine hundred and seventy-two.

2005 Six-Party Joint Statement of Principles

Issued on September 19, 2005, the Joint Statement of Principles proclaims that its parties "reaffirmed that the goal of the six-party talks is the verifiable denuclearization of the Korean peninsula in a peaceful manner." Eventual actualization is contingent on the willingness of North Korea to dismantle its nuclear program and weapons, in exchange for various benefits from the United States, South Korea, Japan, China, Russia. (Head of U.S. delegation Christopher Hill has performed yeoman service in the protracted negotiations.)

Numerous issues need answers before the Statement of Principles can be fully realized, including the following: procedures for North Korean nuclear disarmament; sequence of benefits to North Korea (in conjunction with its disarmament steps); timeline noting when North Korea's "early return" to the Non-Proliferation Treaty (NPT) will take place (which can only be as a non-nuclear weapon state, because North Korea did not attain nuclear weapons before 1967); resolution of North Korea's asserted "right to peaceful use of nuclear energy"; extent of future nuclear inspection of North Korea (will principles of the International Atomic Energy Agency [IAEA] "Additional Protocol" be acceptable to North Korea and satisfactory to other parties?); the possible "provision of a light-water power reactor to North Korea" (redolent of the 1994 Agreed Framework); and steps sufficient to comply with endorsement of undertakings to normalize relations and promote economic cooperation.

The enduring "way out" of such thickets is a nondiscriminatory, worldwide nuclear weapons ban, so that no state could assert (or act on the premise) that another's nuclear weapons necessitate its maintenance of the same.

JOINT STATEMENT OF PRINCIPLES OF SEPTEMBER 19, 2005

For the sake of peace and stability on the Korean Peninsula and in northeast Asia at large, the six parties held in a spirit of mutual respect and equality serious and practical talks concerning the denuclearization of the Korean Peninsula on the basis of the common understanding of the previous three rounds of talks and agreed in this context to the following:

(1) The six parties unanimously reaffirmed that the goal of the six-party talks is the verifiable denuclearization of the Korean Peninsula in a peaceful manner.

The Democratic People's Republic of Korea [DPRK, North Korea] committed to abandoning all nuclear weapons and existing nuclear programs and returning at an early date to the Treaty on the Non-Proliferation of Nuclear Weapons [NPT] and to IAEA safeguards.

The United States affirmed that it has no nuclear weapons on the Korean Peninsula and has no intention to attack or invade the DPRK with nuclear or conventional weapons.

The Republic of Korea [ROK, South Korea] reaffirmed its commitment not to receive or deploy nuclear weapons in accordance with the 1992 Joint Declaration on the Denuclearization of the Korean Peninsula, while affirming that there exists no nuclear weapons within its territory.

The Joint Declaration of the Denuclearization of the Korean Peninsula should be observed and implemented.

The DPRK stated that is has the right to peaceful uses of nuclear energy.

The other parties expressed their respect and agreed to discuss at an appropriate time the subject of the provision of a light-water reactor to the DPRK.

(2) The six parties undertook, in their relations, to abide by the purposes and principles of the United Nations and recognized norm of international relations.

The DPRK and the United States undertook to respect each other's sovereignty, exist peacefully together and take steps to normalize their relations subject to their respective bilateral policies.

The DPRK and Japan undertook to take steps to normalize their relations in accordance with the [2002] Pyongyang Declaration, on the basis of settlement of unfortunate past and the outstanding issues of concern.

(3) The six parties undertook to promote economic cooperation in the fields of energy, trade and investment, bilaterally and/or multilaterally.

China, Japan, the Republic of Korea, Russia and the United States state their willingness to provide energy assistance to the DPRK. The ROK reaffirmed its proposal of July 12, 2005, concerning the provision of 2 million kilowatts of electric power to the DPRK.

(4) Committed to joint efforts for lasting peace and stability in northeast Asia. The directly related parties will negotiate a permanent peace regime on the Korean Peninsula at an appropriate separate forum.

The six parties agreed to explore ways and means for promoting security cooperation in northeast Asia.

(5) The six parties agreed to take coordinated steps to implement the aforementioned consensus in a phased manner in line with the principle of "commitment for commitment, action for action."

(6) The six parties agreed to hold the fifth round of the six-party talks in Beijing in early November 2005 at a date to be determined through consultations.

Response to U.S. Rationale for Nuclear Weapons

Because the United States would be a "prime player" in the elimination of nuclear weapons, this appendix summarizes—and responds to—the fundamental, tripartite rationale for the U.S. arsenal.

First, and most historically rooted, is to reassure member countries of the North Atlantic Treaty Organization (NATO) of the U.S. commitment to their defense. A country's "defense" is for the purpose of "security"; and in a nuclear weapons–free world NATO countries and their populations would no longer be under the shadow of hundreds of ready-to-launch Russian thermonuclear warheads. Furthermore, NATO would no longer need nuclear weapons to "deter" a nuclear attack, because all states would renounce and dismantle their arsenals.

Focusing then on non-nuclear capability, a factor of weight is that Russia for almost two decades now has been shorn of its former Warsaw Pact allies. Another differential from the past is that Russia lost the military and political allegiance of (most of) its 14 former fellow Soviet republics. In addition, Russia in the post-Soviet era does not embrace an ideology—such as "march of communism"—that might conceivably support a reckless, potentially suicidal military quest. Russia, moreover, does not have the non-nuclear military means to prevail or expect to prevail in a sustained offensive drive against "conventional" NATO forces, including those of the United States.

The second major rationale for the U.S. nuclear arsenal is "reassurance of U.S. commitment to their defense" (as with NATO countries), but pertaining to geographically related South Korea, Japan, and Taiwan (Republic of China). Addressing first South Korea, it is regrettable but true that North Korea with its small current nuclear arsenal could destroy Seoul and some other South Korean cities, and thus the North Korean arsenal has an equalizing aspect (which would vanish under worldwide elimination of nuclear weapons). Today, though, even in the best-case scenario of North Korea completing denuclearization and eliminating its arsenal, a *reversal* of that decision in the future would be more easily carried out—geopolitically, legally, and psychologically—under the current six-party process (which focuses solely on North Korea's nuclear program) than under a nonwithdrawal nuclear ban treaty that applies to all countries. An added benefit of such a treaty is that it would enable the United States to relinquish its partially supplicant posture toward the autocratic North Korean government, because a prospective worldwide nuclear ban should and most probably would gain North Korea's accession on the basis of the treaty's equal treatment of states and its liberation of all from the nuclear threat. (Accession to a nuclear ban treaty that requires unanimity for entry into force also can be expected of Iran, which if it currently aspires for nuclear weapons, it likely does so in response to and sustained by Israeli and U.S. nuclear possession.)

Next regarding the island nation of Japan, the U.S. "nuclear umbrella" is deemed useful as a deterrent to possible nuclear assault by North Korea; but any such risk to Japan would be obviated under worldwide elimination of nuclear weapons.

On Taiwan, the problem ostensibly reassured against by the U.S. nuclear arsenal is a presumably non-nuclear attack by China on Taiwan if it "formally declares" independence. (The United States has 20 to 30 times as many nuclear warheads as China, but some Chinese missiles could reach and incinerate U.S. west-coast cities.) If Taiwan ever spurns its U.S. benefactor's strong counsel by formally declaring independence, and if armed conflict ensues, the results would be "less terrible" if the conflict ensued on a different dimension than nuclear war, which would be the ultimate regional or worldwide catastrophe.

With that said, it is most unlikely that Taiwan would heedlessly declare independence; and perhaps with passage of time, China will come to act on the certitude of worldwide goodwill toward China if it voluntarily and nobly acquiesces to Taiwanese independence. Now, however, on the remote chance that Taiwan *does* declare independence and conflict ensues, *should* the United States directly participate when it would have been Taiwan that rejected strong U.S. counsel not to formally declare independence? Based on the longstanding U.S. trepidation about war over Taiwan and the Taiwanese (non-nuclear) military buildup, it seems that the massive U.S. nuclear arsenal has not been extremely reassuring to the United States or Taiwan as a "deterrent." Furthermore, in a world *without* nuclear weapons, China cannot be said to be more likely to attack Taiwan than today, because such a possible attack is predicated not on the existence or nonexistence of nuclear weapons but on the contingency, unlikely as it is, of Taiwan formally declaring independence (against U.S. counsel and absent Chinese acquiescence).

A third major rationale for the U.S. nuclear arsenal is that it may deter attacks by chemical or biological weapons, whether on U.S. soil or against U.S. military forces or friends or allies abroad. A questionable premise here is whether the United States would *ever* use nuclear weapons against a chem-bio attacker, and this is extremely improbable, largely because it would be a disproportionate reaction. Also: in responding to a posited chemical or biological attack, the stellar Armed Forces of the United States could and would respond successfully without introducing the ultimate (nuclear) weapons of mass destruction, nor for that matter with reciprocal use of abhorrent chemical or biological weapons. And, if a worldwide nuclear ban requires prior accession by all states to the CWC and BWC, then any chance of chem-bio assault by a state would be reduced to virtually zero due to the geopolitical impact of unanimity. The risk of chem-bio attack by terrorists would be lessened, in part because terrorists would no longer have potential access (by theft or diversion) to state stocks of chemicals or weaponized biological agents prohibited by the CWC and BWC.

If examined through the lens of a nuclear weapon-free world, much of the rationale for the U.S. nuclear arsenal drops off. And if the dangers of today's nuclear-armed world are taken into account, U.S. and world security will be better served by elimination of nuclear weapons under a treaty with the geopolitical, psychological, and moral force of unanimity.

Notes

CHAPTER 1. THE LANDSCAPE OF NUCLEAR WEAPONS

1. See Lawrence S. Wittner, *Resisting the Bomb: A History of the World Disarmament Movement* (Stanford, CA: Stanford University Press, 1997), II:33. *Resisting the Bomb* recounts the efforts, particularly of grass-roots groups, to lessen the threat of nuclear war and ban nuclear testing (especially atmospheric).

2. Lee Butler, "Keeping Sacred the Miracle of Existence," *Waging Peace Worldwide—Journal of the Nuclear Age Peace Foundation* (Spring 1998): 10. During General Butler's tenure as chief of the Strategic Air Command (1991–1992) and Strategic Command (1992–1994), the United States reduced its nuclear overtargeting of militarily insignificant targets in Russia.

3. "Statement on Nuclear Weapons by International Generals and Admirals," *Arms Control Today*, November-December 1996, 15.

4. Uranium-233, produced in a nuclear reactor using thorium-232 as fuel, could also be used for nuclear weapons. In addition, and although states are not known to have attempted their use, neptunium-237 and americium, which are present in spent nuclear fuel and reprocessing waste, are potential material for the fissile core of nuclear weapon.

5. CANDU (Canadian deuterium-uranium) reactors, 22 of which operate worldwide, are able to sustain fission with natural, unenriched uranium, which is only 0.7 percent readily fissionable isotope uranium-235. CANDU reactors use the "heavy hydrogen" (deuterium) in "heavy water" as moderator; a reactor's moderator absorbs neutrons' energy, slowing them down and increasing their chance of capture by uranium-235 and fission. (An ideal moderator, such as heavy water or purified graphite, has a high neutron cross-section and low absorption cross-section.) Heavy water (or purified graphite) absorbs very few neutrons, so sufficient slow neutrons are available to cause a fission chain reaction using "natural," unenriched uranium fuel, with its mere 0.7 percent uranium-235; and thus a state with such a reactor would not need to master uranium enrichment to produce (unseparated) plutonium (it being a byproduct of uranium fission in reactors). But, heavy water- or

graphite-moderated reactors are *less* worrisome in this respect: a state with such a reactor could forego construction of uranium enrichment facilities, which can produce either LEU (as for light-water-moderated reactor fuel) or HEU, with the latter being the usable nuclear material for a relatively simple gun-type nuclear weapon.

A large, modern power reactor may have a loading of up to 50,000 fuel rods that contain LEU (but LEU can only be a fraction of fuel element composition, lest the uranium melt). The purified ordinary water (i.e., its light hydrogen) used as moderator in these reactors requires fuel enrichment in isotope uranium-235, or else the much more abundant but less fissionable uranium-238 in natural uranium would capture so many neutrons as to prevent the chain reaction.

Distinct from a reactor's moderator are its control rods, which keep the neutron density or "flux" constant in an operating reactor and can shut it down; when fully inserted, the rods' neutron-absorbing material, such as boron, quenches the chain-reaction fissioning of the nuclear fuel (most commonly LEU of 3 to 5 percent isotope uranium-235 enrichment). Heat and radioactivity remain, however, due to decay of fission products.

6. The blast destruction area of the 335-kiloton U.S. W-78 warhead (the mainstay deployment on U.S. Minuteman III ICBMs) is about 20 square miles; thermal-flash burns would extend further.

"In the case of Hiroshima, between 310,000 and 320,000 people were exposed to the various effects of the atomic explosion. Of these, between 120,000 and 150,000 had died by December 1945 and an estimated 200,000 by 1950, if latent effects are included." *Nuclear Weapons—A Comprehensive Study* (New York: United Nations, 1991), 83. Some casualty estimates are not quite as high.

The Nagasaki death toll was horrific but perhaps 30 percent lower, even though the Nagasaki plutonium bomb was about 25 percent more powerful than the HEU bomb dropped over Hiroshima (the Nagasaki explosion was hemmed in by hills, and its epicenter was slightly north of the most densely populated center of the city; both explosions occurred at about 1,800 feet above ground). Japan, for its part, in its bygone militarist days committed cruel aggression and countless atrocities, not least against civilians. But no country is blameless in all history—for example, consider past African-American slavery and Native American mistreatment in the United States, which is still a beacon of human freedom, and whose citizens have contributed so much to the world.

For details of planning and execution of the Hiroshima and Nagasaki missions, see Robert S. Norris, *Racing for the Bomb—General Leslie R. Groves, the Manhattan Project's Indispensable Man* (S. Royalton, VT: Steerforth, 2002), 373–427.

The Soviets, alarmed by events of August 1945, promptly put forth full effort into their own "race for the bomb." The ensuing U.S.-Soviet nuclear build-up resulted in an estimated $200 billion future U.S. cost for environmental cleanup from weapons production and brought deleterious effects to nuclear workers (see Matthew L. Wald, "Work on Weapons Affected Health, Gov't Admits," *The New York Times*, July 17, 1999, A-12).

CHAPTER 2. PARTIAL MEASURES—DE-ALERTING AND NO FIRST USE

1. See Bruce G. Blair, *Global Zero Alert For Nuclear Forces* (Washington, DC: Brookings Institution, 1997).

CHAPTER 3. NUCLEAR BAN ENTRY INTO FORCE

1. China's Vice Premier and Foreign Minister Qian Qichen, at the United Nations on September 15, 1996.

2. "India Shoulders Its Way into Nuclear Club," *The Sun* (Baltimore), May 16, 1998, 7-A.

3. For history and significance of India's nuclear program, see George Perkovich, *India's Nuclear Bomb—Its Impact on Global Proliferation* (Berkeley: University of California Press, 2000).

4. *Proliferation: Threat and Response* (Washington, DC: Office of the Secretary of Defense, November 1997), 15.

5. Brajezh Mishra, "The Evolution of India's Nuclear Policy," *Disarmament Times* (U.N. NGO Committee on Disarmament, Peace and Security), November 1998, 4.

6. Mohammad Azam, press attaché, Pakistani Embassy to the United States, letter to the editor, *The Washington Post*, November 2, 1998, C-6.

7. For book-length coverage of "verification" modalities, highly recommended is the Committee on International Security and Arms Control of the U.S. National Academy of Sciences, *Monitoring Nuclear Weapons and Nuclear-Explosive Materials—An Assessment of Methods and Capabilities* (Washington, DC: National Academies Press, 2005). Many of the verification techniques detailed therein are already in use by the IAEA, which received, along with its director-general, the 2005 Nobel Peace Prize for its important work.

CHAPTER 5. VERIFICATION, DISPOSITION OF HEU, AND REPROCESSING

1. *The United Nations and Nuclear Non-Proliferation*, Blue Book Series (New York: United Nations, 1995), 15.

2. For bi-monthly information and estimates on states' nuclear arsenals and delivery systems, see the Natural Resources Defense Council's "Nuclear Notebook" (Robert S. Norris and Hans M. Kristensen) in *Bulletin of the Atomic Scientists.*

See also Joseph Cirincione, Jon B. Wolfsthal, and Miriam Rajkumar, *Deadly Arsenals: Nuclear, Biological and Chemical Threats* (Washington, DC: Carnegie Endowment for International Peace, 2008).

See also *SIPRI* (Stockholm International Peace Research Institute) *Yearbook* (New York: Oxford University Press, pub. annually).

See also the timely journal *Non-Proliferation Review*.

3. See "Verifying the Deep Cuts Regime," chapter 11 in *The Nuclear Turning Point—A Blueprint for Deep Cuts and De-alerting of Nuclear Weapons*, ed. Harold Feiveson (Washington, DC: Brookings Institution, 1999). The "deep cuts" and de-alerting explored in *Turning Point* would culminate in each nuclear weapon state retaining a maximum of 200 warheads, with most of the remaining warheads off high alert and non-deployed (but still in existence).

See also Steve Fetter, "Verifying Nuclear Disarmament," chapter 3 in *Nuclear Weapons: The Road to Zero*, ed. Joseph Rotblat and Frank Blackaby (Boulder, CO: Westview Press, 1998).

For proposals to strengthen today's nonproliferation regime (which centers on the nonunanimous NPT), see Joseph Cirincione, ed., *Repairing the Regime—Preventing the*

Spread of Mass Destruction Weapons (New York: Routledge/Carnegie Endowment for International Peace, 2000).

4. Cited in Richard Rhodes, *The Making of the Atomic Bomb* (New York: Simon and Schuster, 1986), 535.

5. For recommendations on enhancing "threat reduction" programs, see *Managing the Global Nuclear Materials Threat* (Washington, DC: Center for Strategic and International Studies, 2000).

CHAPTER 6. PROBLEMATIC STATES

1. The planned, to-be-safeguarded power reactors (under the now-defunct Agreed Framework) would not have been proliferation-proof, because light-water reactors do create plutonium as a component of spent fuel; and therefore a state with such a reactor could simply expel IAEA inspectors and proceed with unloading of fuel and separating its plutonium for weapon use.

See Victor Gilinksy and Henry Sokolski, "Those N. Korean Reactors Light Up Danger Signals," *The Washington Post*, August 4, 2002, B-2.

2. See David E. Sanger, "North Korea Says It Has a Program on Nuclear Arms," *The New York Times*, October 17, 2002, A-1.

3. For history of Israel's nuclear program, see Avner Cohen, *Israel and the Bomb* (New York: Columbia University Press, 1998).

4. Even if terrorists could not easily detonate a stolen device due to ignorance of codes of a weapon's "permissive action links" [locks], those mechanisms could possibly be defeated. Or, a warhead could be dismantled and its fissile material (especially HEU, for a relatively simple, gun-type weapon) used in construction of a terrorist weapon, and dissection of a warhead would improve the chances of terrorists successfully fabricating their own.

5. Press conference with Israeli Prime Minister Ehud Olmert, Washington, DC, May 22, 2006.

6. "Commission Begins New Cycle on Nukes, Confidence-Building," *Disarmament Times* (Summer 2000): 1.

CHAPTER 9. PRIOR PROHIBITION OF CHEMICAL AND BIOLOGICAL WEAPONS

1. National Academy of Sciences, Committee on International Security and Arms Control, *The Future of U.S. Nuclear Weapons Policy* (Washington, DC: National Academies Press, 1997), 54.

See also Philip Morrison and Kosta Tsipis, "And Another Thing … Rightful Names," *Bulletin of the Atomic Scientists*, May/June 2003: 7.

2. For subsequent "proposed strategy and techniques" for BWC verification, see Amy E. Smithson, *Resuscitating the BioWeapons Ban—U.S. Industry Experts' Plans for Treaty Monitoring* (Washington, DC: Center for Strategic and International Studies, November 2004).

See also *An International Perspective on Advancing Technologies and Strategies for Managing Dual-Use Risks* (Washington, DC: National Academies Press, 2005).

3. The role of U.S. operatives in creating such a false belief in the Soviet mind centered on a "disinformation" campaign designed to convince the Soviet Union that the

United States was still stockpiling and researching bioweapons, even after Nixon's renunciation of them in 1969. The campaign's goal was to induce the Soviets to expend large efforts and resources toward amassing biological weaponry and agents—which the United States had concluded were unnecessary and of extremely limited military value. But "The [disinformation] campaign undercut Soviet belief in the efficacy of arms control and in the integrity of American policy by misleading Soviet officials into believing that the United States was deliberately violating the Biological Weapons Convention, justify their doing so as well." Raymond L. Garthoff, "Polyakov's Run—When U.S. Intelligence Deceived the Soviets, Were They Being a Bit Too Clever?" *Bulletin of the Atomic Scientists*, September/October 2000, 40.

4. See Nelson Hernandez, "Huge New Biodefense Lab Is Dedicated at Fort Detrick," *The Washington Post*, October 23, 2008, B-4.

5. See Nicolas Isla, "Challenges to the BWTC [BWC] and Some Reasons for Optimism," International Network of Engineers and Scientists Against Proliferation, *Information Bulletin*, April 2008, 70.

For compendium of views on the threat and control of bioweapons, see Susan Wright, ed., *Biological Warfare and Disarmament: New Problems/New Perspectives* (Lanham, MD: Rowman and Littlefield, 2002).

For history of biological weapons and their means of delivery, from antiquity to the present, see Wendy Barnaby, *The Plague Makers—The Secret World of Biological Warfare* (New York: Continuum, 2000).

CHAPTER 10. RESERVATIONS

1. Former Senator Bob Dole offered a crucial eleventh-hour endorsement of the CWC, and Senator Richard Lugar, among others, worked strenuously for its adoption.

2. Russia's implementation of the CWC 10-year period (from 1997) for elimination of Russia's chemical weapons has lagged from the start, as has (to a somewhat lesser extent) U.S. chemical elimination. The extension of time now claimed by and accorded to the two countries informs the importance of an appropriately lengthy nuclear ban timetable for eliminating nuclear weapons, and the separate deadline, perhaps extending beyond weapons elimination, for blending down of HEU to LEU—although HEU *use* would be terminated, and all HEU stocks consigned to international safeguards, six months before the end of the nuclear ban weapons-elimination period. (The physical dismantling of nuclear weapons is relatively simple and much easier than safely incinerating the 40,000 or so tons of reactive, hazardous chemical weapon agents possessed by both the Russia and the United States when the CWC entered into force in 1997.)

CHAPTER 11. COUNTERING NEAR-EARTH OBJECTS

1. Supposing the improbable, that is, that the nuclear ban's executive council did not approve a request by, say, the United States to develop one or a few "nuclear explosive devices" to attempt to destroy or divert a fast-approaching NEO, then the United States would be justified in proceeding if accompanied by a message such as this: "We are developing these nuclear explosive devices for use to meet the imminent NEO threat.

The fabrication process and all other aspects will be entirely transparent, with specific invitation for representatives of all permanent nuclear ban executive council members [the pretreaty nuclear powers] to continuously monitor the undertaking."

2. *Nuclear Weapons—A Comprehensive Study* (New York: United Nations, 1991), 67.

3. Zeljko Ivezic, Serge Tabachnik, Roman Ratikov, et al. "Solar System Objects Observed in the Sloan Digital Sky Survey Commissioning Data," *Astronomical Journal*, November 2001, 2749-2784.

CHAPTER 12. SOCIETAL VERIFICATION

1. The permanent members of the nuclear ban's executive council would be the five most-longstanding nuclear weapon states (which are also today's NPT nuclear weapon states), as well as Israel, India, Pakistan, North Korea, and any other state(s) that are possessors of nuclear weapons at the time of the treaty's entry into force.

Non-nuclear weapon states should not object to this distinction between permanent and nonpermanent council members, because all states would be members of the nuclear ban's conference of all parties, and all would have their turns on the executive council. Furthermore, any state at any time could bring a concern directly to the council (or, if deemed necessary, directly to the world).

CHAPTER 13. OTHER MATTERS

1. Editorial, *Disarmament Times*, April 1998, 1.

2. Daisaku Ikeda, "1999 Peace Proposal," *Living Buddhism*, April 1999, 42. Daisaku Ikeda, the recipient of 245 academic honors, is president of Soka Gakkai ("Value-Creation Society") International (SGI), which has developed and sponsored/co-sponsored the acclaimed exhibition *Nuclear Arms—Threat to Humanity*, held in 24 cities worldwide. (Other SGI exhibitions include *Human Rights in Today's World* and *The Courage to Remember—Anne Frank and the Holocaust*, the Japanese version of the Simon Wiesenthal Center's Holocaust exhibition.)

The first two Soka Gakkai (Japan) presidents, Tseunesaburo Makiguchi and Josei Toda, were imprisoned by World War II Japanese militarist authorities, Makiguchi unto his death, for opposing the regime's abnegation of religious freedom.

For views on attainment of peace and elimination of nuclear weapons, see David Krieger, president, Nuclear Age Peace Foundation, and Daisaku Ikeda, *Choose Hope* (Santa Monica, CA: Middleway Press, 2002).

3. Douglas Roche, *The Ultimate Evil—The Fight to Ban Nuclear Weapons* (Toronto: Lorimer, 1997), 68. (Although nuclear weapons are the ultimate, indiscriminate destroyers of life, this does not mean that states or citizens of states that possess nuclear weapons can therefore be imputed as "evil"—in the absence of a worldwide nuclear weapons ban.)

Pope Benedict has said, "The truth of peace requires that all—whether those governments which openly or secretly possess nuclear arms, or those planning to acquire them—agree to change their course by clear and firm decisions, and strive for a progressive and concerted nuclear disarmament." (Message on "World Peace Day," December 8, 2005).

4. Statement by 117 international civilian leaders, issued at the National Press Club, Washington, D.C., February 2, 1998.

5. For peerless delineation of Ronald Reagan's longstanding desire to eliminate nuclear arms, see Paul Lettow, *Ronald Reagan and His Quest to Abolish Nuclear Weapons* (New York: Random House, 2005).

On July 8, 1986, President Reagan said that he was encouraged that Gorbachev had "actually proposed reducing the number of weapons and has also voiced the opinion that our goal should be the total elimination of nuclear weapons. Well, that's been our goal for forty years. In fact, I was campaigning on that in 1980—that I supported and would support and hope that we could see the end of nuclear weapons—total elimination" (*Quest*, 194).

6. Former German Chancellor Helmut Schmidt has said, "[T]he INF treaty was the end of the Cold War." Quoted in Jonathan Schell, *The Gift of Time* (New York: Metropolitan Books, 1998), 123. (*The Gift of Time*, by the author of *The Fate of the Earth*, recounts dialogues with political, ex-military, and scientific notables on nuclear abolition and approaches to it.)

The landmark Reagan-Gorbachev INF treaty was signed in December 1987 and saw the destruction of a combined 2,692 U.S.-Soviet ballistic and cruise missiles, completed in May 1991; the treaty covered ground-launched missiles of greater than 500 kilometers, and less than a 5,000-kilometer range. (In his second Inaugural Address on January 21, 1985, President Reagan declared, "We seek the total elimination one day of nuclear weapons from the face of the earth.")

7. *The Writings of Nichiren Daishonin* (Tokyo: Soka Gakkai, 1999), 1:1125.

CHAPTER 14. SUMMARY

1. Interview, *Newsweek*, December 3, 2001, p. 32.

APPENDIX A: ANALYSIS OF THE MODEL NUCLEAR WEAPONS CONVENTION

1. Lawyers Committee on Nuclear Policy, 675 Third Avenue, Suite 315, New York, NY 10017 (www.lcnp.org). See links for Model Nuclear Weapon Convention text in English plus Arabic, Chinese, French, Russian, and Spanish versions.

2. Text of the Advisory Opinion (*Legality of the Threat or Use of Nuclear Weapons*), plus judges' dissenting and separate opinions, is available at http://64.22.89.210/~ialana/?q=worldcourtproject#icj.

3. A main international contact for the Abolition 2000 Global Network to Eliminate Nuclear Weapons (www.abolition2000.org) is the Nuclear Age Peace Foundation (www.napf.org).

Index

"Agreed Framework," 40–42
"Agreement on Destruction and Non-Production to Facilitate the Chemical Weapons Convention," 67
Algeria, 1
ally protection, 114–15
anthrax, 59
Argentina, 1
arms race history, 2
asteroid, 76–78
Atoms for Peace program, 86

"baseline inventories," 24
Belarus, 1
the Bible, 87
biological weapons, 1, 59, 64–65; renunciation of, 12; response to, 116; and treatment, 59. *See also* Biological Weapons Convention
Biological Weapons Convention (BWC), 7, 58, 59, 61–65, 107–11; joining of, 84; withdrawal from, 61–63
Bohr, Niels, 24
bombers, 8–9
Brazil, 1

Britain, 1, 3, 28; nuclear-powered military vehicles and, 30; test bans and, 10; warhead elimination, 49
Bush, George H. W., 86–87
Bush, George W., 2, 87, 91
Butler, Lee, 3

Canada, 28
Carter, Jimmy, 86
Central Intelligence Agency, 68
"challenge inspections": chemical weapons and, 58, 72; nuclear weapons and, 25–28
chemical weapons, 1, 59, 60–61, 63; ban verification, 58; protection against, 68–69; renunciation of, 12; response to, 116. *See also* Chemical Weapons Convention
Chemical Weapons Convention (CWC), 7, 47, 58–59, 61–65, 86; inspections, 68; joining of, 84; Russia and, 68; United States and, 67–75; withdrawal from, 61–63
Chemical Weapons Convention Implementation Act, 72

China, 1, 3, 41, 115; No First Use and, 9;
   test bans and, 10
classified information, 24, 73
Cold War, 2, 64
comets, 76–78
Comprehensive Test Ban Treaty (CTBT),
   10–11, 13
Conference on Disarmament (C.D.), 85
Cooperative Threat Reduction, 87
"crime against humanity," 82

"de-alerting," 8–9; shortcomings, 9
declaration of weapons. *See* weapons
   declaration
"discriminatory" treaty terms, 21
disinformation campaign,120–21 n.3
domestication legislation: chemical
   weapons and, 73–74; criminality of
   proliferation and, 81, 89; Nuclear Ban
   Treaty and, 84, 95

Egypt, 63
Eisenhower, Dwight D., 86
energy supply, 34–35, 36, 42–43. *See also*
   nuclear energy; peaceful nuclear
   assistance
entry into force: delay, 85, 91; Model
   Nuclear Weapons Convention and,
   94–95; proposed Nuclear Ban Treaty
   and, 10–11, 13–15, 84

false-alarm launch, 8
"final disposal," 34–37
First Use Policy, 9
fissionable material, 4, 28–34; declaration
   of, 46, 84, 95, 96; final disposal of,
   34–37; ownership of, 35–36; replacement, 50–51; reprocessing of, 34–37;
   transportation of, 37–38; safeguards
   and, 22, 29, 31, 33, 35–38. *See also*
   highly enriched uranium; low-enriched
   uranium; plutonium; uranium
France, 1, 3, 10, 28; nuclear-powered
   military vehicles and, 30
"future states," 99–100

"general" destruction, 6
the Geneva Protocol, 60

"geopolitical enemies," 2, 9, 45–46,
   114–15
geopolitical force, 25, 30, 50, 91,
   114–15
Germany, 28
Gorbachev, Mikhail, 2, 86
"gun-assembly" weapon, 3,
   6, 11

Hague Conference (1899), 60
highly enriched uranium (HEU), 3, 4, 6,
   22; blending down of, 7, 29; declarations, 25; monitoring of, 31; reduction,
   29–30; research reactors, 33. *See also*
   low-enriched uranium; Nuclear Ban
   Treaty, proposed
Hiroshima detonation, 6, 118 n.6
hostilities, localized, 7
"hydrogen" bomb, 2, 5

Ikeda, Daisaku, 86
"implosion" weapon, 3, 5–6
India, 3, 45; Non-Proliferation Treaty and,
   6; and Pakistan, 12; test bans and,
   11–12
INFCIRC/152 (IAEA), 22–23
INFCIRC/225 (IAEA), 37–38
INFCIRC/540 (IAEA), 25, 26
inspection rejection, 72–73. *See also*
   Nuclear Ban Treaty, proposed
intercontinental ballistic missiles
   (ICBMs), 8
Intermediate-Range Nuclear Forces
   Treaty, 86
International Association of
   Lawyers Against Nuclear Arms,
   93. *See also* Model Nuclear Weapons
   Convention
International Atomic Energy Agency
   (IAEA): documented measures,
   22–23, 25, 26; safeguards, 22–23,
   37–38, 40
International Court of Justice, 93
Iran, 43
Iran-Iraq war, 60–61
Iraq, 26–28
Israel, 1, 3, 45; Non-Proliferation Treaty
   and, 6; warhead elimination, 49

Italy, 28
Itoh, Iccho, 5–6

Japan, 28, 35, 40, 41, 115
Joint Statement of Principles, 42

Kazakhstan, 1
Kennedy, John F., 86
Khan, A. Q., 11

Libya, 1
Limited Test Ban Treaty (LTBT), 10
low-enriched uranium (LEU), 7, 28–29, 31–34, 99, 117–18 n.5

"managed access," 25–28
"mass destruction," 59–60
medical isotope production and, 33
Model Nuclear Weapons Convention (MNWC), 93–94, 100; chem-bio weapons and, 96–97; entry into force and, 94–95; reprocessing and, 99; timetable for, 97; verification measures for, 98; withdrawal from, 97
"Moscow Treaty," 1–2, 3, 87

Nagasaki detonation, 5–6, 118 n.6
"national security exception," 73–74
Near-Earth Asteroid Rendezvous (NEAR), 77
Near-Earth Object (NEO), 76–78, 121–22 n.1
Nichiren, 87
Non-Proliferation Treaty (NPT), 6–7, 9, 86, 92, 101–6; amendments, 53, 54; challenge inspections, 26; discriminatory terms, 21; inadequacies, 54; material accountability and, 22; safeguards, 23; withdrawal, 17–18, 41, 52. See also NPT non-nuclear states; NPT states
non-states, 13, 14
non-withdrawal provision, 18–21
North Atlantic Treaty Organization (NATO), 114
North Korea, 1, 3, 40–43, 114–15; Non-Proliferation Treaty and, 6

NPT non-nuclear states, 22, 26, 36, 44, 52. See also specific states
NPT states, 49, 53–54. See also specific states
nuclear abolition forum, 85
nuclear abolition process, 85–86. See also Nuclear Ban Treaty, proposed
Nuclear Ban Treaty, proposed, 13–16, 21, 38–39, 55–56, 85–86, 88–91, 122 n.1; chem-bio weapons ban and, 61–63; entry into force, 14; financing, 56; future states and, 99–100; highly enriched uranium use under, 30–33; inspections, 25–28, 31, 33, 36, 90; International Atomic Energy Agency role, 23; internationally controlled stockpiles under, 77–78; low-enriched uranium fuel under, 31–34; material breach of, 20, 43, 89; medical isotope production and, 33; Near-Earth Objects and, 76–78; noncompliance, 24–25, 31–32, 36, 43–44, 80, 89, 91; nondiscriminatory aspects, 42; non-membership, 44–45; non-withdrawal and, 17, 18–21, 89; no reservation policy, 66–67, 71, 74–75; reprocessing and, 34–37; research reactors and, 33; safeguards, 29, 31, 35, 36–38, 90; societal verification, 80–83; timetable, 33, 37, 47–51, 84, 88, 89, 97–98; unanimous accession, 14–15; verification process of, 21, 23–28; voluntary accession, 38, 44; weapons elimination, 47–51, 84–85. See also Model Nuclear Weapons Convention; Non-Proliferation Treaty; nuclear ban verification
nuclear ban verification, 21, 23, 28, 33, 36, 90; baseline inventories and, 24–25; challenge inspections and, 25–28; cost of, 56–57; managed access and, 25–28. See also Nuclear Ban Treaty, proposed
nuclear blast, 5–6
"nuclear disarmament," 53
nuclear energy, 6, 36, 55. See also nuclear power reactors; peaceful nuclear assistance

nuclear material. *See* fissionable material; nuclear weapons

nuclear navies, 30–33

nuclear power reactors, 4, 30, 117 n.4, 117–18 n.5; conversion of, 31; ownership of, 35–36. *See also* peaceful nuclear assistance; peaceful use

Nuclear Threat Initiative, 28

nuclear weapons: "boosted," 5; consequences of, 60; dismantling of, 1, 24; elimination, 47–51, 53; engineering of, 3–5; military renunciation of, 3; state renunciation of, 1; testing, 1; use of, 5–6. *See also* Nuclear Ban Treaty, proposed

nuclear weapons states, pre-1967, 6–7. *See also* Britain; China; France; Russia; United States

"Organization for the Prohibition of Nuclear Weapons," 25

Pakistan, 1, 3, 45–46, 48, 49; and India, 12; Non-Proliferation Treaty and, 6; test bans and, 11, 12; warhead elimination, 49

peaceful nuclear assistance, 6, 23, 40, 69–70. *See also* nuclear energy

peaceful use, 6, 36, 55, 78

"permitted withdrawal," 7

plutonium, 4–5, 22, 29, 34; declaration, 25; diversion, 42; production, 4–5; reprocessing, 32, 34–37; safeguards, 37; use, 5–6

poison gas, 60. *See also* chemical weapons

"preemptive" attack, 7, 41

problematic states, 40–46

Putin, Vladimir, 87

radiation, 5–6

rationale for nuclear weapons, 114

reactor spent fuel, 34–35

Reagan, Ronald, 86, 123 n.5

refurbishment, 50

"regional nuclear weapon-free zone," 52

renunciation of chem-bio weapons, 12, 62, 64, 67–68, 75

renunciation of nuclear weapons, 36; by the military, 3; by the state, 1

research: highly enriched uranium reactors and, 33, 90; nuclear reactor fuel and, 35

research reactors, 33

reservations, 66–67, 75, 89

reward fund, 80

Russia, 1–3, 41, 46, 114; Chemical Weapons Convention and, 68, 121 n.2; de-alerting and, 8; First Use Policy of, 9; highly enriched uranium and, 34; nuclear-powered military vehicles and, 30; plutonium and, 37; weapons elimination and, 48. *See also* "Moscow Treaty"; Soviet Union

safeguards: fissionable material, 22, 29, 31, 33, 35–38; International Atomic Energy Agency and, 22; Non-Proliferation Treaty, 23; Nuclear Ban Treaty, proposed, 29, 31, 35, 36–38, 90; plutonium, 37

seismic monitoring, 10, 11–12

Six-Party Joint Statements of Principles, 112–13

Six-Party Talks, 41, 42–43

societal verification, 79, 80–83

South Korea, 40, 41

sovereignty, 18

Soviet Union, 1, 120–21 n.3; biological weapons and, 64; test bans and, 10. *See also* Russia

spiritual implications, 87, 89

"Stardust" mission, 77

Stevenson, Adlai, 2

stockpiles, internationally controlled, 77–78

Strategic Arms Limitation Talks (SALT I and SALT II), 86

Strategic Arms Reduction Treaty (START I), 2, 86–87

Strategic Offensive Reductions Treaty (SORT). *See* "Moscow Treaty"

submarines, nuclear powered, 8–9, 30

supreme interests, 18

Taiwan, 1, 115

terrorism, 29, 92, 116. *See also* terrorist warhead acquisition

terrorist warhead acquisition, 3–4, 7

test explosions, 1; atmospheric, 10; underground, 10, 11

thermonuclear bomb. *See* "hydrogen" bomb

thorium-based fuel, 35

threat reduction funds, 28

Threshold Test Ban Treaty, 10

treaties: for arms reduction, 2; biological weapons and, 7; chemical weapons and, 7; discriminatory terms of, 21; for non-proliferation, 6–7, 40, 90–91; for reduced nuclear deployment, 1–2; termination of, 54–55; for testing limitations, 10; United States and, 86–87; violation, 80, 91; withdrawal from, 7, 17–21, 41, 61–63, 97. *See also specific treaties*; "Agreed Framework"; Model Nuclear Weapons Convention; Nuclear Ban Treaty, proposed; unanimous accession

Treaty on the Non-Proliferation of Nuclear Weapons. *See* Non-Proliferation Treaty

treaty violation reporting, 80

Ukraine, 1

unanimous accession: Comprehensive Test Ban Treaty and, 13–14; Model Nuclear Weapons Conference and, 94–95; Nuclear Ban Treaty, proposed, 14–15

United Nations: biological weapons ban and, 64; charter articles, 18–19; discussion document, 93; dues scale, 56; elimination of nuclear weapons role, 13–14, 18–19, 20, 46, 85; nuclear safeguards and, 23; stockpiles of, 77–78

United Nations Disarmament Commission conference, 46

United Nations Security Council Resolution 1441, 26–28

United States, 1–2, 120–21 n.3; chem-bio weapons and, 61, 64–65, 116; Chemical Weapons Conference and, 67–75; Congress, 71–72; de-alerting and, 8; defense budget, 56; First Use Policy of, 9; highly enriched uranium and, 34; Israel and, 45; and North Korea, 40–43; nuclear-powered military vehicles and, 30; plutonium and, 37; presidential policy on WMD treaties, 86–87; rationale for nuclear weapons, 114–16; reservation policy, 66–67, 70–71; test bans and, 10, 11; threat reduction programs, 28; treaty procedure and, 15, 70–72; weapons elimination and, 48; weapons renunciation, 3 whistle-blowers, 81, 83. *See also* "Moscow Treaty"

uranium, 4. *See also* highly enriched uranium; low-enriched uranium

Vajpayee, A., 11

Vienna Convention of the Law of Treaties, 15, 16, 19, 20, 50, 54, 90–91; reservations, 66

warhead, 47

wars, bulwark against, 7

weapons declaration, 24–25, 84, 95, 96

weapons delivery systems, 99

weapons elimination, 47–51, 89, 98

whistle-blowers, 80–81; asylum for, 81

Yarkovsky Effect, 76

About the Author

FREDERICK N. MATTIS has been an independent scholar of nuclear and chem-bio weapons for over twenty years. He is a graduate of St. John's College in Annapolis, Maryland.